The Essential...
Lady Gaga

Published in 2024
by Gemini Editions Ltd
Part of the Gemini Books Group

Based in Woodbridge and London

Marine House, Tide Mill Way,
Woodbridge Suffolk, IP12 1AP
United Kingdom

www.geminibooks.com

ISBN 9781917082433

A CIP catalogue record for this book is available from the British Library.

Every reasonable effort has been made to trace copyright-holders of
material reproduced in this book, but if any have been inadvertently
overlooked the publishers would be glad to hear from them.

Printed in Turkey
10 9 8 7 6 5 4 3 2 1

The Essential...
Lady Gaga

UNOFFICIAL AND UNAUTHORIZED

ANNIE ZALESKI

Contents

OPPOSITE
Lady Gaga, 2010.

Introduction

The history of pop music is driven by bold iconoclasts. Take Lady Gaga, the artist born Stefani Germanotta on March 28, 1986. Her stage name is a reference to Queen's 1984 hit "Radio Ga Ga," a song that doubles as an ode to the days when musical greats dominated the airwaves. She's an avowed fan of The Beatles and David Bowie—the latter's 1973 LP *Aladdin Sane* is a favorite—and also counts as inspirations Led Zeppelin, Cyndi Lauper, Bruce Springsteen, and Billy Joel. More importantly, because Gaga grew up learning from these superstars, she intuitively understands what makes pop icons tick: constant creative reinvention, deep self-confidence, and a willingness to be brave.

Not everyone has the fortitude to be this fearless, which is why true pop stars are few and far between. Yet Gaga seemed destined to revolutionize music. When she released her debut, 2008's *The Fame*, her presence launched an entirely new pop era—one predicated on supersonic dance-pop that drew on the then-red-hot EDM movement as well as older trends such as electroclash and punkish disco. Gaga's voice was as brassy and expressive as a Broadway performer's, but she exuded genuine warmth and a cheeky vibe. Who else could sing about wanting to take a spin on someone's "disco stick" with a straight face?

Gaga subsequently amassed a loyal fanbase because of her unicorn-caliber range and open-minded approach to music. Her albums hover around a sonic sweet spot—electro-pop calibrated for marathon dancefloor sessions—but also make room for the occasional power ballad, twangy rock number, or rustic country

THE ESSENTIAL... LADY GAGA

OPPOSITE TOP
Making an entrance
at the 2010 Brit
Awards.

**OPPOSITE
BOTTOM LEFT**
As Jo Calderone
performing onstage
with Queen's Brian
May, 2011.

**OPPOSITE BOTTOM
RIGHT** At the Met
Gala, 2019.

ABOVE Singing
a tribute to Julie
Andrews at the
Academy Awards,
2015.

melody. Her collaborations, meanwhile, span pop greats, rock gods, and hip-hop stars; she's the rare artist that can nail a heartfelt tribute to *The Sound of Music* at the Oscars, go toe-to-toe with Metallica during a snarling Grammy Awards collaboration, or team up with crooner Tony Bennett. Even critically-maligned-at-the-time efforts such as 2013's *ARTPOP* have proven to be both influential and beloved—a sign that Gaga is always ahead of the curve.

Onstage and in the studio, her innate charisma collided with musical theater-kid quirkiness and long-smoldering ambition; she was the consummate outsider finally crashing the mainstream pop party, doing fancy her own way and dishing out cutting lyrical observations. Smartly, Gaga fed off of the delicious tension generated by being a misfit permeating the elite world of celebrity and popularity, as if she were a character in an eighties teen movie. She acknowledged the dark side of celebrity—not for nothing did she title a 2009 expanded reissue of her debut album *The Fame Monster*—but nevertheless embraced the glitzy excess she critiqued.

And while other stars might be accused of hypocrisy for such a move, Gaga escaped disapproval by leaning into the utter absurdity of being famous. Her fashion was *Jetsons* couture—dramatic makeup, gravity-defying wigs, impractical shoes, space-age costumes—but also unexpected. She wore a disgusting-but-brilliant dress made from raw flank steak at the 2010 MTV Video Music Awards and showed up at the Grammy Awards in an egg-shaped cocoon, from which she later emerged to sing "Born This Way."

Yet she also understood that her newfound fame and celebrity could be used for good. Led by the title track, an instant-classic pride anthem that encourages people to be their fully authentic selves, the 2011 album *Born This Way* signaled Gaga's move into advocacy for the LGBTQIA+ community. The following year she and her mother, Cynthia, co-founded the Born This Way Foundation, a youth-oriented nonprofit that remains dedicated to helping promote kindness and mental health.

Such empathy also informs her acting forays. While she's portrayed herself on many TV shows, Gaga has drawn on her

theater experience and live musical performances for compelling character work. She won a Golden Globe for her role as the murderous Countess in *American Horror Story: Hotel*, and she drew raves for her portrayals of aspiring songwriter Ally Maine in a 2018 remake of *A Star Is Born* and Patrizia Reggiani in 2021's *House of Gucci*.

Pop music could (and should) be a serious creative endeavor—but Gaga knew pop stardom itself didn't have to be so serious and that she could be refreshingly weird and unpredictable. Simply put, it's her colorful, inclusive planet; we're just lucky enough to be able to visit occasionally and soak up some of her shimmer. Here's how she became the beloved Mother Monster, the patron of nonconforming pop artists everywhere.

CHAPTER ONE

THE
BEGINNING

PAGE 12 Lady Gaga, 2008.

OPPOSITE Posing in an origami dress designed by Glenn Hetrick, 2008.

As a toddler, Stefani Joanne Angelina Germanotta, the New York City native who years later became the glamorous jet-setting pop star Lady Gaga, was mesmerized by the possibilities of a piano owned by her parents. "When Stefani started to crawl, she would use the leg of the piano to pull herself up and stand, and in doing so, her fingers would eventually land on the keys," her mom, Cynthia, was quoted as saying in news stories about a high-profile 2016 auction for the instrument. "She would stay there and just keep pressing the keys to hear the sound. We would then start to hold her up or sit on the bench and let her tinker."

In an early indication of her singular talent, this tinkering was fruitful. Gaga learned to play the piano by ear, a fact Cynthia discovered after asking her daughter if she wanted lessons. "She said that she heard the music in her head," Cynthia later recalled to *InStyle*. "She didn't understand why she had to take a lesson." Like many kids, Gaga hated practicing piano, but the lessons paid off. Inspired by the cash register sounds at the beginning of Pink Floyd's "Money," the budding composer carefully plotted out and composed her first-ever song called "Dollar Bills" on Mickey Mouse-themed staff paper.

Unlike many famous musicians, Gaga didn't have parents who earned a living in the entertainment business. Dad Joe started and later sold a successful company, GuestWiFi, that provided Wi-Fi to hotels, while Cynthia worked for the telecom giant Verizon. Crucially, however, her parents provided a foundational musical education. On the family's living room record player, her classic rock-loving dad spun albums by Billy Joel, Pink Floyd, The

Rolling Stones, Queen, David Bowie, and Led Zeppelin. Gaga also became a massive fan of The Beatles, and later got a tattoo of a peace sign on her left wrist in honor of the city's *Imagine* memorial to John Lennon. And, in a nod to the family's Italian-American heritage, opera superstar Andrea Bocelli and Frank Sinatra's *Duets* were also in heavy rotation. "I had a really amazing childhood," she recalled in an early 2008 interview. "A lot of culture, a lot of meatballs, a lot of marinara."

Rocker Bruce Springsteen was an even bigger touchstone for young Gaga. Not only did she soak up lyrical and thematic inspiration from "The Boss," but his music also inadvertently helped her advance in her career. One Christmas, the teenaged Gaga received a Springsteen songbook for the piano. Her dad made her a tantalizing offer: learn to play her favorite song, 1975's "Thunder Road," and they would get a baby grand piano. By this time, Gaga had been taking piano lessons for years, but learning "Thunder Road" was a challenge since it was so different from the classical pieces she was used to performing. Yet she eventually mastered it—and onward she went.

Gaga paired her classic rock grounding with a love of flashy pop icons, like eighties superstars Cyndi Lauper and Michael Jackson. She also gravitated toward strong women in the music industry, such as Shirley Manson, the Scottish firebrand leading the nineties alt-rock group Garbage, and Debbie Harry, the iconic frontwoman of NYC avant-garde punks Blondie. The latter group is an early blueprint for Gaga's career. The band were music video innovators—in fact, they filmed clips for every song on 1979's *Eat to the Beat*, creating a video album long before it was a common method of promotion—and Debbie Harry was an influential fashion icon who embraced both DIY punk couture and high-fashion sophistication.

ABOVE Lady Gaga's parents, 2010.

OPPOSITE TOP The peace tattoo seen on her left wrist is in honor of John Lennon.

OPPOSITE BOTTOM In 2010 with Bruce Springsteen, one of Gaga's musical heroes.

THE ESSENTIAL... LADY GAGA

However, Gaga was also very much a child of the nineties MTV generation. During the height of the teen-pop movement driven by *NSYNC and Britney Spears, she and friends would head for Times Square after school and stand in the crowd outside of MTV's offices while *Total Request Live* was filming, in the hopes of catching a glimpse of the day's guest stars. In a prescient example of foreshadowing, the MTV Video Music Awards were also must-see TV for a young Gaga.

By the time she hit adolescence, Gaga had also honed an offbeat fashion sense. In kindergarten, she went the DIY route for her costume when she acted in *Three Billy Goats Gruff*, fashioning billy goat horns "out of tinfoil and a hanger," she told *The Guardian*. Gaga also pretended to dress up when watching the MTV Video Music Awards by draping a cozy, hand-knitted afghan around her body and imagining it was fancy formalwear. Perhaps even more important, she learned that being fashionable involved hard work and sacrifice: In high school, she took a job as a waitress in a diner; one of her first splurges after starting to get paid was a Gucci purse.

ABOVE Female-led bands, Blondie (L) and Garbage (R) were an inspiration for Gaga.

THE ESSENTIAL... LADY GAGA

When Gaga reached high school, her career ambitions started to crystallize. At age fourteen, she connected with Don Lawrence, a voice teacher who counted celebs such as Christina Aguilera, U2's Bono, and Mick Jagger as clients. As a high school freshman, she also formed and fronted a classic rock cover band that favored songs by Led Zeppelin, U2, Pink Floyd, and Jefferson Airplane. Gaga's mom also accompanied her to New York City clubs, where the aspiring talent honed her solo act.

Despite her prodigious (and precocious) talent, Gaga was also a normal, quasi-rebellious teenager. She dated an older man, had a fake I.D., and would party downtown on weekends. Teachers also chided her for wearing low-cut shirts that revealed too much cleavage, and she got a tattoo of a G-clef on her lower back. But this wild child behavior didn't dampen her ambition; along with practicing music, she also took acting classes from the renowned Lee Strasberg Theatre & Film Institute, learning intense method-acting skills that would later become integral to her music career. "She was always extremely driven, extremely hardworking," her mom said in *The Daily Beast*. "If she had to go to a voice lesson and her friends wanted to hang out, they wouldn't always understand. With her, it was a passion. Not a hobby."

Like many artistic, ambitious, and talented kids, Gaga suffered due to her single-minded devotion to the performing arts. "Let's say that she was uniquely very different growing up and her peers didn't always appreciate that," her mom told *InStyle* years later. "As a result, she experienced some meanness and cruelty at various times—things like being taunted, isolated, humiliated, both in school and out of school." A classmate later recalled that older girls mocked Gaga in secret ("They always talked behind her back, like, 'Gross, she's the Germ! She's dirty!'"); Gaga herself says she was also teased for her looks: having a big nose, an intense self-tan, and a penchant for sculpting dramatic eyebrows.

Not everyone remembers Gaga as being a misfit, however. "She was always popular," Julia Lindenthal, who attended a nearby high school, told *New York*. "I don't remember her experiencing any social problems or awkwardness." (Gaga didn't name names, but in a 2011 *Rolling Stone* interview, she refuted quotes from former classmates talking up her popularity: "All of those people were bullies! Perhaps it's their way of trying to redeem themselves.")

"She was always extremely driven, extremely hardworking. If she had to go to a voice lesson and her friends wanted to hang out, they wouldn't always understand. With her, it was a passion. Not a hobby."

CYNTHIA GERMANOTTA

James Phillips, who taught at nearby Regis High School, remembered a memorable play where the crowd cheered and screamed in reaction to Gaga's performance. "It wasn't something she tried to incite," he told *TODAY*. "Even though it wasn't her own songs, everyone recognized that she was talented and exceptional even for a high-school kid."

And if some of her peers begrudged her talent, others recognized that she was going places. When Gaga held a sixteenth birthday bash, attendees received a demo featuring some of her original songs as a parting gift. It made quite an impression. "Everyone was playing her demo, like, 'Whoa, she's going to be a star,'" Justin Rodriguez, a Regis High School graduate, told *New York*. "She was by far the most talented person in high school, but she'd do so many random acts of kindness, like saying, 'Your singing has gotten so much better, you're working hard and I've noticed.' She wasn't a diva at all."

Despite her early achievements, Gaga had a long way to go before she attained the stardom she so craved. Little did she know then what a wild and unexpected path her life would take.

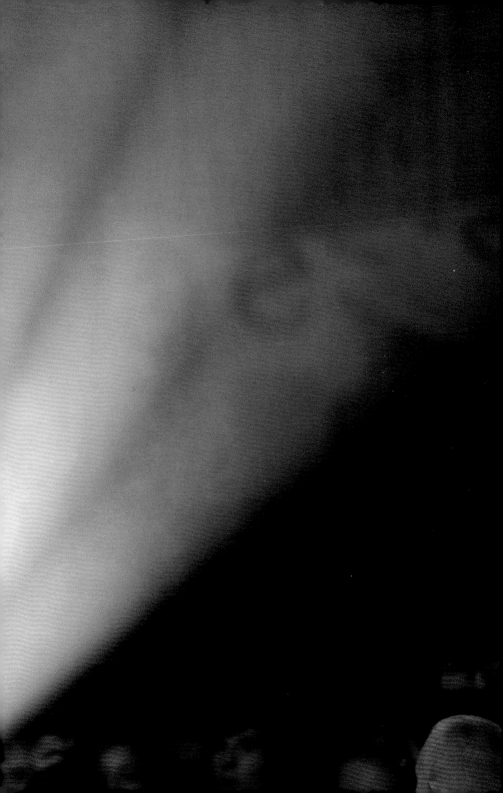

CHAPTER TWO

STEPS
TO STARDOM

Stefani Germanotta didn't just snap her fingers one day and transform into Lady Gaga. First, she embraced one of the biggest teenage rites of passage: going to college. At age seventeen, Gaga was one of twenty students picked for the prestigious musical theater conservatory called the Collaborative Arts Project 21 (CAP21), which was then affiliated with New York University's Tisch School of the Arts. She entered the program during the 2004–2005 school year and studied art history and music.

In March 2005, she performed two original songs at an NYU cancer benefit, UltraViolet Live. Sporting a strapless green top and a long white skirt, she displayed intense concentration while playing and singing at the piano. The first song, "Captivated," was an earnest love ballad; her second choice, "Electric Kiss," was brisker and more dramatic, with Gaga pounding on the keys forcefully. As a video of the benefit shows, college freshman Gaga wasn't yet an out-of-this-world pop star. "She was a very suburban, preppy, friendly, social party girl," an ex-dorm-mate anonymously told the *New York Post* in 2010. "There was nothing that would tip you off that she had this Warhol-esque, 'new art' extremism."

But even if her fashion sense hadn't yet developed its edge, her ambition was already in full bloom. In April, Gaga performed a solo acoustic set opening for the pop-rock band Nada Surf at the South Street Seaport; a month later, she played gigs at the punk dive CBGB and the Lower East Side club Pianos. By this time, the school year was over, and she had turned her attention to playing out as much as she could.

The summer after her freshman year of college was pivotal for

THE ESSENTIAL... LADY GAGA

her musical development. Gaga rented an apartment at Stanton and Clinton on the Lower East Side and started finagling bookings at New York City music venues using every trick in the book, like pretending to be her own PR rep. Paul Colby and Kenny Gorka, who co-owned Greenwich Village club The Bitter End, saw Gaga's talent even without her sleight of hand; in fact, the club became something of a second home for her, and she regularly performed there. At this point, Gaga's music was quite different—"bittersweet rock ballads to power-pop rock," as she put it in her early bio.

By fall 2005, school had lost its allure, and she decided to take time off from NYU and focus on her music career. Her parents weren't necessarily thrilled, but they supported her decision, with

OPPOSITE TOP
Gaga studied at The Tisch School of the Arts from 2004–2005.

OPPOSITE BOTTOM
Legendary Greenwich Village club The Bitter End, where Gaga honed her live performances.

ABOVE Nada Surf, 2003. Gaga opened for the rock band in the early days of her career.

one condition: She had a hard deadline of one year to make things happen and land a record deal. Gaga quickly got to work.

Within weeks of leaving NYU, she put together The Stefani Germanotta Band (sometimes called SGBand) with bassist Eli Silverman, drummer Alex Beckmann, and guitarist Calvin Pia. The group had a "really dingy practice space" that was "under some grocery store, where you'd have to enter through those metal doors on the sidewalk," Pia told *The New York Observer*. Back then, Gaga herself "was very bubbly, very eccentric, very driven," he added, noting she'd drag her gigantic keyboard to the space from her nearby apartment. "The high art thing? I did not see any hints of that!"

In October 2005, Gaga and the full band debuted at The Bitter End and continued to perform around New York City venues such as the Knitting Factory and The Lion's Den. Vintage footage of the group performing Led Zeppelin's "D'yer Mak'er" at The Bitter End in early 2006 is laid-back and jammy. Gaga sounds soulful, but she channels her inner Robert Plant as the song progresses.

A five-song demo called the *Words* EP also captures the band's sound during this period. The tunes are well-wrought and catchy,

but they aren't necessarily easy to pick out as Gaga songs. While her vocal power is evident, the musical style is all over the map, encompassing mid-tempo piano ballads ("Wish You Were Here"—not the Pink Floyd song), Broadway-esque ("Something Crazy"), and funky blues-rock ("No Floods"). That EP was followed in March 2006 by another EP, *Red and Blue*.

Her hard work and constant gigging paid dividends. In spring 2006, she started working with the New Jersey producer Rob Fusari, who co-wrote Destiny's Child's "No, No, No" and also co-produced the trio's "Bootylicious." The two met purely by chance, via an artist by the name of Wendy Starland, who happened to be part of a songwriters showcase at the Cutting Room that also featured Gaga. Starland was impressed by the headliner's poise and vocal prowess.

As it turns out, Starland was already working with Fusari, and he had given her a quest: Find him a female artist that could be the figurehead of a rock band like The Strokes. Gaga didn't necessarily fit the bill; in fact, Fusari told *New York* his first impression was that she was "a Guidette, totally *Jersey Shore*." However, Gaga's charisma

THE ESSENTIAL... LADY GAGA

and flair were undeniable, and she convinced him to open his mind and embrace a different kind of New York talent. "I thought she was a female John Lennon, to be totally honest," Fusari told *New York*. "She was the oddest talent." Gaga and her dad teamed up with Fusari to form a company, Team Love Child, to handle her music career development.

From there, she started diligently commuting from New York City to Fusari's studio in Parsippany, New Jersey. They'd work together seven days a week, with lunch breaks at the chain restaurant Chili's to regroup and recharge. Together, the musician and producer started making "a very heavy rock record... hard and grungy," he told *Billboard*. However, the direction wasn't quite jelling—until Fusari saw what Nelly Furtado had done to turn her career fortunes around: evolve from doing hip-hop-tinged folk songs such as 2000's "I'm Like a Bird" to sleeker, beat-heavy tunes such as "Promiscuous" with Timbaland.

"My antenna went up," Fusari explained to *Billboard*. "I said, 'Stef, take a look at this. I'm really an R&B guy. I never produced a rock record in my life. I don't know, you think maybe we should shift gears?'" Gaga was reluctant at first and protested the change, but Fusari's persuasive arguments won out. "I finally got her to agree, and that day we did 'Beautiful, Dirty, Rich,' which was me sitting at an MPC drum machine and Stef playing her piano riff."

> "I thought she was a female John Lennon, to be totally honest. She was the oddest talent."
>
> ROB FUSARI

"Beautiful, Dirty, Rich" is a far cry from her solo piano work: Its neon-hued pop vibe sounds fresh—a collision of mainstream sass and edgy New York City dance grooves. Gaga would later claim in a June 2008 interview she "was doing a lot of drugs" when she wrote the song, although you can already pinpoint the themes she'd explore on *The Fame* coming together very coherently. "Whoever you are or where you live, you can self-proclaim this inner fame based on your personal style, and your opinions about art and the world, despite being conscious of it," she said, and noted the song also critiqued Lower East Side poseurs. "There was a lot of rich kids who did drugs and said that they were poor artists, so it's also a knock at that."

It was in this period that Stefani Germanotta started going by Lady Gaga. As might be expected, the origin stories vary for her name and persona. In one version, the moniker was said to be inspired by a nickname derived from Queen's 1984 hit "Radio Ga Ga." In another telling, Fusari sang "Radio Ga Ga" to her in the studio; when he attempted to text her the song's title, his phone's auto-correct somehow changed it to "Lady Gaga," and she ran with it. To muddy the waters further, the *New York Post* claimed in 2010 the name "Lady Gaga" was developed in a marketing meeting.

At any rate, Gaga's music and presence were finally starting to attract attention from record labels. Fusari slipped her demo to Island Def Jam, which called Gaga in for an audition. Oozing self-assurance and wearing white thigh-high boots and a black minidress, she sat down at the piano and wowed everyone. "The way she played and the lyrics and the way she acted and sang was just so different and in your face, and you couldn't turn away," Joshua Sarubin, who worked in A&R for the label, told *NJ.com*. "She had this presence like, 'I'm sexy and I don't care what anybody has to say about it.'"

"The way she played and the lyrics and the way she acted and sang was just so different and in your face, and you couldn't turn away."

JOSHUA SARUBIN, ISLAND DEF JAM

Label head Antonio "L.A." Reid was also bowled over during the audition, as he later recalled to *Access Hollywood*, "When she was done, I said, 'You are an amazing artist, a true star, and you will change music,' and I signed her."

The label seemed like a good home, but unfortunately, the honeymoon period was short-lived. Gaga's tenure on the label was distinguished not by demo time or development help, but by Reid's disinterest. "She'd want to sit in a room with him and talk about her music, and he just wouldn't do it," Fusari recalled to *Billboard*. "We still don't know why." With little fanfare, Island Def Jam dropped her.

After she became a star, Reid later admitted he regretted his decision, blaming his change of heart on the fact he was "having a bad day" and telling *Access Hollywood* that cutting her loose "was the worst thing I've ever done." However, the damage was done, and a devastated Gaga retreated to her Lower East Side apartment to lick her wounds, smarting at the thought her chance at stardom had disappeared. "I was so depressed," she told *New York*. "That's when I started the real devotion to my music and art."

CHAPTER THREE

BECOMING GAGA

PAGE 36
Lollapalooza, 2007.

OPPOSITE Gaga's
early mentor, DJ
Lady Starlight,
pictured in 2009.

In hindsight, this post-record deal period was both the wildest and most transformative time of Lady Gaga's life. In photos taken in the 2006–2008 era, you can trace her evolution from an ambitious piano-rock prodigy to a no-holds-barred glam-rock 'n' roller. This reinvention also illustrated her resilience. Despite the massive setback of a lost record deal, she poured her heart and soul into music and creativity—and pushed herself to embrace the kind of fearlessness needed for pop stardom.

Speaking to *The Independent* in 2009, Gaga recalled a particularly rough performance where the crowd was chatty and rude. Fueled by "a couple of drinks" and fired up by her new songs and an "amazing outfit," she all but demanded they pay attention to her. "I sat down, cleared my throat and waited for everyone to go quiet. It was a bunch of frat kids from the West Village and I couldn't get them to shut up. I didn't want to start singing while they were talking, so I got undressed. There I was sitting at the piano in my underwear. So they shut up." Gaga added that this snap decision to disrobe was a turning point: "I made a real decision about the kind of pop artist that I wanted to be. Because it was a performance art moment there and then."

Gaga also started go-go dancing at New York City's dive bars, which were dominated by "a lot of nerdy, record-collecting DJs" and club kids, she said in an early 2008 interview. "People have personas; the nightclubs feel like a culture. The music is underground, but it's also mainstream." Her musical taste also expanded during this time: She got heavily into glam, especially genre icons such as T. Rex and Cockney Rebel ("It's a sub-set

ABOVE Glam icons such as Cockney Rebel (pictured) had a profound impact on Gaga's evolution as an artist.

of all these things I love: cabaret, burlesque, metal, rock," she told *The Guardian*), and also rekindled her long-standing love of Queen and David Bowie; the latter's 1973 LP *Aladdin Sane* was a heavy-rotation favorite. She also became "fascinated with Eighties club culture," she told *Rolling Stone*, as well as more cutting-edge alternative acts: gloomy post-punk band The Cure, synth-pop icons Pet Shop Boys, and modern electro-pop act Scissor Sisters.

These inspirations had a profound impact on her evolution as an artist and the music she was starting to explore. "When I was playing the New York rock clubs, a lot of record labels thought I was too theatrical," she told the *Daily Mail*. "Then when I auditioned for stage musicals, the producers said I was too pop."

However, during this period, her friendship group also expanded exponentially. She started hanging out with Justin Tranter, who fronted the glam-kissed rock band Semi Precious Weapons and would later become a successful pop songwriter. Gaga also started dating Lüc Carl, the manager of the Lower East Side dive bar St. Jerome's, who drove a green Camino and was once described as having "loud Nikki Sixx hair." The pair would be in each other's

THE ESSENTIAL... LADY GAGA

ABOVE Lady Gaga
(far right) walks
onstage at the
Slipper Room,
New York in 2007.
Gaga's raunchy
variety shows there
were the start of
her evolution as a
performance artist.

lives on and off for years, and Carl would inspire Gaga songs all the
way through 2011's *Born This Way*.

At St. Jerome's, Gaga also met and befriended a performance
artist/go-go dancer named Lady Starlight, a fan of glam and
heavy metal who became a mentor and formative influence. "I'll
never forget when she turned to me one day and she said, 'You're
a performance artist,'" Gaga told *Rolling Stone*. "I was like, 'You
think so?' When people believe in you, that's what makes you grow."

For Gaga, this support system arrived at the perfect time, as
she was exploring new sounds, new identities, new fashions. "They
gave me a sense of belonging somewhere," she confessed to *Rolling
Stone*. "It'll make me cry just talking about it, because when you
feel so much like you don't fit in anywhere, you'd do anything just to
make a fucking friend. And when I met the right people, they really
supported me."

Still, Gaga was trying to come into her own as capital-G
Gaga. "She was wearing a version of [the eventual Gaga look],"
Starlight said to the *New York Post*. "Definitely spandex, for sure,
some kind of unitard, but casual. She still looked abrupt and out

of place." Creatively, the women put together a wild, raunchy variety show, becoming known for setting hairspray on fire during a revue that also drew on burlesque, electroclash, and other out-there performance art moves. "There was all these singer/songwriter girls like Alanis Morissette and Norah Jones," Lady Starlight later told *TODAY.* "And we were all turntables, keyboards, and bikinis. The tourists were staring full on."

At this point, Gaga's fashion sense was heavily influenced by what was going on around her in the Lower East Side. She also started making her own outfits because it was more affordable, mixing and matching fabrics such as leather and sequins, even as she admired the luxe style and cuts of fashion greats: Fendi, Versace, Gucci, Dolce & Gabbana. As

she mused in 2008, the mix of low-brow culture and high fashion posed a challenge: "How do you make five dollars look like five grand? How do you feel like five grand when you've got five bucks in your pocket?"

ABOVE Lüc Carl, Gaga's on-again-off-again boyfriend.

Fusari was less than impressed when he saw Gaga's revue with Lady Starlight, telling *New York*, "It was *Rocky Horror* meets eighties band, and I didn't get it at all. I told Stefani that I could get her another DJ, but she was like, 'I'm good.'" Gaga's father also wasn't necessarily thrilled to see his daughter onstage in outfits such as a leopard-print G-string and a black tank top. "It wasn't 'She's inappropriate' or 'She's a bad girl' or 'She's a slut,'" she told *Rolling Stone*. "He thought I was nuts, that I was doing drugs and had lost my mind and had no concept of reality anymore."

Admittedly, he may have had reason to worry, as Gaga later confessed she was partying and overindulging during this period. To *Rolling Stone* journalist Neil Strauss, she revealed her apartment had bedbugs and roaches, as well as "mirrors with cocaine everywhere. [I had] no will or interest in doing anything but making music and getting high." In a separate *Rolling Stone* interview,

THE ESSENTIAL... LADY GAGA

ABOVE Supporting
New Kids on the
Block in 2008.

she stressed her parents and childhood had nothing to do with
her debauched behavior; instead, she was emulating some of her
heroes. "All of the things I went through were on my own quest
for an artistic journey to fuck myself up like Warhol and Bowie
and Mick, and just go for it. All of the trauma I caused to myself.
Or it was caused by people that I met when being outrageous and
irresponsible."

Still, Gaga's drive never wavered. In August 2007, she performed
an early morning set at the major music festival Lollapalooza. In
hindsight, the performance is charming: The crowd looks like they
have *no idea* what to make of Gaga, who struts her stuff in front of
the stage through disco-punk jams "Dirty Ice Cream" and "Disco
Heaven" and steps behind a keyboard for more introspective
moments. Her outfit is also delightfully oddball: She sports a disco
ball bra, high stockings, and skimpy underwear.

Despite his skepticism about her new direction, Fusari still
believed in Gaga. He connected her with his frequent producer
collaborator, Vincent Herbert, who had worked with R&B stars
Destiny's Child and Toni Braxton and had a label imprint,

> # "I was in such a dark space in New York. I was so depressed, always in a bar. I got on a plane to L.A. to do my music and was given one shot to write the song that would change my life and I did."

Streamline Records, with ties to Interscope Records. With the blessing of the latter's Jimmy Iovine, Herbert signed Gaga, giving her a second chance at major label stardom.

She crossed paths with rapper Akon, who was working with a producer called RedOne. Akon was duly impressed by her vocal and songwriting skills and signed Gaga to his label, KonLive. (The imprint was also affiliated with Interscope Records; Gaga ended up releasing albums jointly through Streamline and KonLive.) "When I see a star, I just know it," he recalled to *Entertainment Weekly* in 2018. "From the moment she walked in [for our first meeting], her appearance and her attitude felt brand new and fresh."

In spring 2008, the world heard their first official music from Lady Gaga: "Just Dance." Co-written with RedOne, who also produced the song, the song came together in just ten minutes in the studio. Although "Just Dance" was almost given to the Pussycat Dolls, Gaga recorded it herself, and the rest is history. The song hit No. 1 in Australia and Canada, and it became a dance club hit in the US, performing well enough that Gaga nabbed the opening slot on the comeback arena tour by eighties teen-pop heartthrobs New Kids on the Block.

The single "saved my life," Gaga told *The Guardian* in 2009. "I was in such a dark space in New York. I was so depressed, always in a bar. I got on a plane to L.A. to do my music and was given one shot to write the song that would change my life and I did." She never looked back—quite literally. "I left behind my boyfriend, my apartment. I still haven't been back. My mother went in and cleared it for me."

CHAPTER FOUR

JUST DANCE

PAGE 46 Onstage at the Q102 Jingle Ball, 2008.

OPPOSITE Lady Gaga at the MTV Studios, 2008.

Lady Gaga was predisposed to thinking about art in a grandiose way, and as *The Fame* era unfolded, she increasingly used the noted artist, photographer, writer, and raconteur Andy Warhol as a guiding light. "My music is pretty much a reflection of my transition from New York uptown to New York downtown, and all the things that I've discovered," she said in a 2008 interview. "I'm making pop records about an underground lifestyle."

And so, in addition to all the synth-stacked dance music, the album encompasses new wave ("I Like It Rough"), disco-pop ("The Fame"), electro-soul ("Starstruck"), and hip-hop ("Paper Gangsta"). There's even a piano ballad, "Brown Eyes," that doesn't feel far removed from the music she was doing in college. Describing *The Fame* to MTV UK, she elaborated: "You've got club bangers to more 70s Glam to more singer-songwriter records to rock music. *The Fame* is not about who you are—it's about how everybody wants to know who you are."

The latter statement certainly reflects Gaga's not-so-secret desire to be known by everyone the world over. But thematically, her music took provocative stances about fame and celebrity—an outsider's view of what it means to be part of society's elite—and wrestled with fame's dualities and contradictions. "Money Honey" toasts to fame—and celebrates the glitz and glam that comes with it—but realizes it's not what matters; instead, passionate kisses are a much better, worthier goal. On "Paper Gangsta," which she wrote about the pain of losing her Island Def Jam record deal, she admits the promised land isn't so shiny, and further vows not to get involved with people who don't support her.

The layers of meaning in "Paparazzi" are even more compelling, and hint at more complex songwriting yet to come. "On one level it is about wooing the paparazzi and wanting fame," she said in her official bio that came with *The Fame*. "But it's not to be taken completely seriously. It's about everyone's obsession with that idea." The song was also said to be inspired by her relationship with Lüc Carl, which makes sense given her next point: "[The song is] also about wanting a guy to love you and the struggle of whether you can have success or love—or both."

Elsewhere, "Poker Face" addressed her bisexuality—she told one audience it was about hiding your lascivious thoughts about a woman because you're with a man—and "LoveGame" boasts indelible lines about riding on a "disco stick." In an interview with *Rolling Stone*, she quipped the naughty phrase is "another of my very thoughtful metaphors for a cock," dreamt up one night while she was out clubbing.

That song came together during a productive January 2008 week in California at the famed Record Plant with co-collaborator RedOne. In addition to "LoveGame," she polished off two other big hits: "Just Dance" and "Poker Face." As she later told *Rolling Stone*, "I just felt so free, and there was nothing in my way." Fittingly, *The Fame* itself was done in a tidy thirty days—a staggeringly short timeline that included mixing and mastering.

But although her ambitions were lofty, she still had a long way to go to become a success. *The Fame* was released in late October 2008 in the US and sold a modest 24,000 copies its first week in stores. Still, December 2008 was one of Gaga's most formative months yet. She released a holiday song, "Christmas Tree," and received her first Grammy Award nomination, with "Just Dance" in the running for Best Dance Recording. She also met Bruce Springsteen at the Z100 Jingle Ball held at Madison Square Garden. "I climbed over the seats and gave him a big hug, and he told me I was sweet," Gaga

THE ESSENTIAL... LADY GAGA

told *Rolling Stone*. "Then I had a massive breakdown—I cried on the man's neck!"

Gaga's rocket ride to the top was just beginning. In the UK, "Just Dance" spent three weeks at No. 1 in early 2009. Not long after, acclaimed synth-pop duo Pet Shop Boys enlisted her to sing Dusty Springfield's iconic contribution to their 1987 hit "What Have I Done to Deserve This?" at the Brit Awards. Wearing a stage outfit that made her resemble an Alice in Wonderland-surreal teacup, she carried herself like a poised veteran while dueting with vocalist Neil Tennant.

After spending the end of 2008 gaining steam, "Just Dance" also topped the US *Billboard* Hot 100 in January 2009. The song took a staggering twenty-two weeks to hit the top spot, and it stayed there for three weeks—a nice consolation since "Just Dance" missed out on winning its Grammy, losing the Best Dance Recording category to Daft Punk.

Gaga launched her first headline trek, The Fame Ball Tour, in March 2009. Speaking to MTV News, she teased that the show was an immersive, multi-sensory experience. "It's going to be as if you're walking into New York circa 1974," she said. "There's an art installation in the lobby, a DJ spinning your favorite records in the main room, and then the most haunting performance that you've ever seen on the stage."

Gaga was hands-on with planning the night, overseeing every aspect to ensure the party lived up to her exacting expectations. Her insistence on making personal sacrifices for her art would become her calling card in the years to come, as would her workaholic tendencies. However, the extra effort paid off, as The Fame Ball Tour was an eye-popping multimedia extravaganza with top-notch stage props. For example, she commissioned frequent collaborator Tom Talmon Studio to make a literal (light-up) disco stick. "It looks like a giant rock-candy pleasuring tool," she noted lightly to *Rolling Stone*.

ABOVE Sydney, Australia, 2009. Gaga creates her own bubble dress using British designer Hussein Chalayan as inspiration.

As The Fame Ball Tour marched onward, Gaga proved "Just Dance" was no fluke. In April 2009, she had another US No. 1 hit with "Poker Face," which topped the *Billboard* Hot 100 for one week and also became a global hit. The "Poker Face" video shows off a different, more put-together version of Gaga—the confident pop star, not the reformed club kid. Fittingly, the clip takes place at a fancy mansion with a pool, with party scenes involving beautiful people playing high-stakes strip poker and making out. Gaga's outfits are also slicker: skintight vinyl with spike heels, an electric-blue leotard with strategic cut-outs, her disco ball-encrusted glasses, a blunt-cut blonde wig.

Gaga also started branching out during TV performances, drawing on her background in theater and classical music. A May 2009 appearance found her performing "Paparazzi" as a forceful acoustic piece, sitting with her legs crossed at a clear piano. This version was dramatic and theatrical, like a show-stopping cabaret number, and oozed confidence. For this performance, she wore a bubble dress, constructed by sewing buoyant clear balls to a leotard;

THE ESSENTIAL... LADY GAGA

the net result was that she resembled a bunch of transparent grapes. Gaga dubbed this a "bubble installation" and noted it was based on a dress the British designer Hussein Chalayan had presented in a previous runway show.

The bubble dress reappeared again during Fame Ball Tour live performances, though she made it clear that these out-there fashions had multiple layers of meaning beyond simply wanting to look different. "The methodology behind [my crazy looks] is when they wanted me to be sexy and they wanted me to be pop, I always fucking put some absurd spin on it that made me feel like I was still in control," she said in the 2017 documentary *Gaga: Five Foot Two*, and told *Rolling Stone* in 2009, "I don't feel that I look like the other perfect little pop singers. I think I look new. I think I'm changing what people think is sexy."

> "The methodology behind [my crazy looks] is when they wanted me to be sexy and they wanted me to be pop, I always fucking put some absurd spin on it that made me feel like I was still in control."

Being freed from conventions was the best thing for her creativity. However, her outward confidence wasn't always the same as her inward reality, and this 2009 era was rough for her self-esteem; among other things, critics could be brutal when writing about Gaga, and she was a public spectacle due to her outfits. "It was like I was being bullied by music lovers, because they couldn't possibly believe that I was genuine," she told *Rolling Stone*. "I was too different or too eccentric to be considered sincere."

Gaga was also dealing with some tough personal worries while navigating being in the public eye. Her dad's health had started to deteriorate after years of living with a malfunctioning aortic valve, but he was resisting getting the open-heart surgery that would've fixed the issue. Depressed and unable to come home from tour, she instead channeled her sadness and anxiety into a string-laden, throwback power ballad, "Speechless," that nods to Elton John's lush arrangements and harmonies. Gaga sent the song to her dad, which seemed to have done the trick: Much to her relief, her dad had the needed procedure in October 2009.

Despite these scares, her professional life continued to soar. In June, "LoveGame" became her third Top Five hit in the US. In September, she won three awards overall at the MTV Video Music Awards, including Best New Artist, and performed a dramatic version of "Paparazzi." She also showed off her acting skills during her *Saturday Night Live* debut, appearing in the recurring club/ dance spoof sketch "Deep House Dish" alongside guest star Madonna. The women played up their (fake) rivalry, play-fighting and tossing insults at each other.

Weeks later, "Paparazzi" would become her fourth Top Ten US single, reaching No. 6 on the *Billboard* Hot 100. The song featured her most elaborate music video yet. Directed by Jonas Åkerlund and co-starring actor Alexander Skarsgård as Gaga's boyfriend, the clip starts with Skarsgård pushing Gaga over a balcony in a fit of anger. She survives and comes back to life using a wheelchair and then space-age crutches. Throughout the video, Gaga wears a variety of outrageous outfits as she plots out her revenge and warns of fame's hubris. At the end, she sports a skin-tight yellow bodysuit with cartoonish mouse heads (think a cross between deadmau5 and

ABOVE Making her *Saturday Night Live* debut in a spoof sketch with Madonna (R), in 2009.

THE ESSENTIAL... LADY GAGA

Mickey Mouse) and sunglasses with multiple circular lenses. Calmly, and with absolutely no remorse, she poisons Skarsgård—finally achieving the infamy she craves.

After the elaborate video for "Paparazzi," the upscale fashion world took notice of her creativity and potential. "Gaga had some archival pieces from Thierry Mugler, but after 'Paparazzi,' everything changed," an ex-associate told *New York*. "It happened in the blink of an eye. Suddenly, every fashion designer in the world was e-mailing her images."

As the year wound down, more good news emerged: Gaga was nominated for multiple Grammys, including Song of the Year and Record of the Year for "Poker Face" and the prestigious Album of the Year for *The Fame*. Still, even at this early stage, she demonstrated creative restlessness—and a strong desire to avoid Warhol's fifteen-minute fame trap. "I feel like I have so much to do," she told *Rolling Stone* in 2009. "The whole world sees the number-one records and the rise in sales and recognition, but my true legacy will be the test of time, and whether I can sustain a space in pop culture and really make stuff that will have a genuine impact."

CHAPTER FIVE

THE FAME
MONSTER

PAGE 58 The Monster Ball Tour live in Los Angeles, California, 2009.

OPPOSITE Playing "EMMA," an instrument that includes a bass guitar, a synthesizer, and a drum machine custom made by Glenn Hetrick.

On January 31, 2010, Lady Gaga won her first two Grammy Awards: Best Dance/Electronica Album for *The Fame* and Best Dance Recording for "Poker Face." Gaga also opened the awards show with a barn-burning performance. Wearing a sea-green Armani leotard with puffed shoulders and fins at her hip—making her look like a whimsical fish—she danced first to "Poker Face" and then dueted with Elton John on her "Speechless" and his "Your Song."

For the latter part of her Grammy Awards performance, she played a Baldwin piano customized by Terence Koh, featuring arms with claw-like hands protruding from the top. Although the instrument resembled something out of a horror movie—say, newly minted zombies thrusting their arms up from the ground—the arms actually represented her fans. The decor was deeply meaningful, as Gaga's had amassed an army of loyal fans dubbed "Little Monsters."

Thanks to a blockbuster 2009 and *The Fame*, the Little Monsters fanbase started to grow and take on a life of its own. Gaga's proclamations of misfitdom and being an outsider resonated deeply: Her fans created art, wore elaborate costumes to concerts, and mimicked their idol's stage moves, such as the claw-like paw she'd throw up like a sign of solidarity. They would also have visceral reactions to her music and lyrics, picking up on the deeper themes and finding solace (and solidarity) in Gaga's honesty.

Still, it was clear she viewed the musician-fan dynamic as a mutually beneficial relationship. "When I wake up in the morning, I feel just like any other insecure 24-year-old girl," she told *Rolling Stone*. "But I say, 'Bitch, you're Lady Gaga, you better fucking get up and walk the walk today,' because they need that from me. And they inspire me to keep going."

Gaga kept the Little Monsters satisfied with the late 2009 release of *The Fame Monster*, which ended up being somewhere between an addition and a sequel to *The Fame*. As the title implies, her inspiration was quite different this time around: darker, more ominous, slightly scary. She had been watching horror films and 1950s science fiction movies; as a result, she pointed out one of the more overlooked facets of horror movies: "If you notice in those films, there's always a juxtaposition of sex with death. That's what makes it so scary. Body and mind are primed for orgasm and instead somebody gets killed."

Although *The Fame* and *The Fame Monster* share collaborators, including RedOne and Space Cowboy, the music is already edging into another galaxy. There's the slow-burning power ballad "Speechless," of course, as well as nods to high-stepping Broadway razzmatazz ("Teeth"), sultry ballroom dancing ("Alejandro"), and eighties dance-pop ("Dance in the Dark"). Gaga's newer songs also exude greater lyrical sophistication and depth. "Dance in the Dark" illuminates heartbreak by noting that the concept of dancing in the dark seems to be a cover for insecurities and an imperfect relationship. "Telephone," a song Gaga originally wrote for Britney Spears's *Circus* album, captures the agony and ecstasy of miscommunication (or no communication), while the *de facto* title track, "Monster," likens an all-consuming romantic relationship to getting entangled with a zombie.

Fittingly, the aesthetic for the cover of *The Fame Monster* is darker and less polished. The EP features a black-and-white photo of Gaga hugging a black vinyl jacket around herself while wearing a blunt-cut, triangular blonde wig. Unlike the star-kissed visage seen on *The Fame*, her look here is solemn and mysterious.

"It's yin and yang. It's 'This is how I feel. I feel divided. I feel a dichotomy within myself. I am ready for the future, but I mourn the

ABOVE Lady Gaga performs live onstage in Los Angeles, California, during her Monster Ball Tour, 2010.

OPPOSITE TOP At the Trent FM Arena, Nottingham, UK, 2010.

OPPOSITE BOTTOM Dueting with Elton John (L) on a custom-made piano at the 2010 Grammy Awards. The zombie-esque arms represent Gaga's fans, Little Monsters.

THE ESSENTIAL... LADY GAGA

THE ESSENTIAL... LADY GAGA

PAGE 64–65 Lady
Gaga, 2010.

OPPOSITE TOP
With Beyoncé in
the music video for
"Telephone".

OPPOSITE BOTTOM
Gaga plays one
of several keytars
especially made
for the Monster Ball
Tour, Birmingham, UK.

past," she explained. "And it's a very real rite of passage—you have to let go of things. You have to mourn them like a death so that you can move on, and that's sort of what the album is about."

The videos for this album also upped Gaga's game, starting with the clip for lead single "Bad Romance." She worked with Francis Lawrence, who directed 2007's *I Am Legend*, on a compact look at Gaga's themes from this era: the perils of fame, female empowerment, revenge, and atonement, embracing the spotlight on your own terms. Setting-wise, it's a cross between a sci-fi film set in the distant future and a James Bond-caliber espionage film, along with a dash of fashion world drama.

The nine-minute cinematic epic "Telephone" was even more elaborate. Directed by Jonas Åkerlund, who also helmed the clip for "Paparazzi," the video finds Gaga and Beyoncé updating the story of Bonnie and Clyde, as seen through the noir lens of Quentin Tarantino. (Beyoncé's character is named "Honey Bee"—a *Pulp Fiction* reference—and Tarantino was so into the video's plot and theme he lent the crew the Pussy Wagon from the film *Kill Bill: Volume 1*.)

In November 2009, Gaga launched The Monster Ball Tour to support *The Fame Monster*. In many ways, it was a bigger, more expansive version of The Fame Ball Tour. For example, she had several oversized pyramid-shaped keytars that were described by artistic collaborator Glenn Hetrick as "almost M.C. Escheresque" in design. "And we did a clear version with internal blacklighting and we did a purple version of that," he explained to *SciFi Vision*. Her disco stick was now a blazing disco torch with strobe light capabilities.

Conceptually, The Monster Ball Tour was a "pop-electro opera" with a broad scope and a cohesive plot built around a theme of "evolution," which she said hewed to what *The Fame Monster* itself was about. "I don't write about fame or money at all on this new record," she told *Rolling Stone*. "So we talked about monsters and how, I believe, that innately we're all born with the monsters already inside of us—I guess in Christianity they call it original sin—the prospect that we will, at some point, sin in our lives, and we will, at some point, have to face our own demons, and they're already inside of us."

As the tour progressed, Gaga also collected more awards and accolades. "Bad Romance" topped the charts in Canada and the UK, and peaked at No. 2 in the US, Australia, and New Zealand, while "Telephone" also topped the UK singles charts, giving Gaga her impressive fourth No. 1 to date there. Three years after her low-key daytime set, she headlined Lollapalooza.

And on September 12, 2010, she wore her controversial meat dress to the MTV Video Music Awards, where she was nominated a record-setting thirteen times and won eight awards. An outfit so infamous that it has its own lengthy Wikipedia entry, the dress was worn in solidarity with gay members of the US military impacted by the "Don't ask, don't tell" policy. As she explained to Ellen DeGeneres after the show: "It is a devastation to me that I know my fans who are gay... feel like they have governmental oppression on them. That's actually why I wore the meat tonight. If we don't fight for our rights, pretty soon we're going to have as much rights as the meat on our bones."

Overseen by Argentine designer Franc Fernandez and Gaga's stylist Nicola Formichetti, the thirty-five-pound carnivorous concept came together in a week, and was made from matambre, a thinly sliced cut of beef Fernandez bought from his family's favored butcher shop. "Working with meat as a material requires you to do it last minute," Fernandez told *StyleList*; in fact, the dress had to be pieced and sewn together while Gaga was wearing it. "We didn't get a chance to have a fitting," he told *Huffington Post*. "The only time she had it on was for the VMAs. Only when I saw it in the monitor did I know it would be big."

Gaga certainly turned heads when she accepted the award for Video of the Year for "Bad Romance" from Cher while wearing the outfit. But this acceptance speech was also memorable because Gaga gave fans an official tease of *Born This Way*, announcing the album's title and singing a snippet of the title track.

Gaga performed "Born This Way" at the Grammy Awards in early 2011, the same year *The Fame Monster* won the Grammy Award for Best Pop Vocal Album, while "Bad Romance" won two awards: Best

Female Pop Vocal Performance and Best Short Form Music Video. However, this night was even more memorable for Gaga's mode of transportation: Instead of strutting down the red carpet, she was carried in an egg-like vessel by several muscular shirtless men. The contraption was designed by Hussein Chalayan, the same visionary that inspired her high-concept bubble dress.

She remained in the vessel through her performance of "Born This Way." The egg glowed slightly as it was wheeled onstage and then opened to reveal Gaga, who "hatched" out of it and immediately put on a flat-brimmed hat. Later, Gaga told radio host Ryan Seacrest she spent seventy-two hours in the plexiglass egg—which was temperature-controlled—leading up to the performance. "It was a very creative experience," she said. "It was time for me to really prepare and think about the meaning of the song and get prepared for the performance."

Living in an enclosed space for days on end is certainly a nod to her background in method acting—but also points to her single-minded artistic vision. Indefatigable optimism and creativity—it's the Lady Gaga way.

CHAPTER SIX

BORN
THIS WAY

PAGE 70 Lady Gaga live onstage during her Born This Way Ball Asia tour, 2012.

OPPOSITE
With creative collaborator, Nicola Formichetti (L) arriving at Maxim's de Paris, France, 2011.

While on The Monster Ball Tour, Gaga began work on a new album. She started pairing her usual sassy, savvy soundbites with earnest political and social activism. She also started looking back and analyzing the origins of her past destructive behaviors, in hopes of finding understanding and healing. One of her realizations was that being bullied growing up had a deeper impact than she had appreciated.

"It was something so painful," she says. "This huge wound that had been inside of me for so long that I had buried in drugs and alcohol and older men and over and over in a cycle of just unhappiness with myself and looking outward to fix it, to numb it."

The result of this soul-searching is *Born This Way*, which was more declarative and defiant than the music she had released to date. "*Born This Way* is my answer to many questions over the years: Who are you? What are you about?" she told *The Metro* newspaper. "The most paramount theme on the record is me struggling to understand how I can exist as myself as someone who lives halfway between fantasy and reality all the time."

If this seems like an extension of *The Fame Monster*, that's partly true—but instead of scary movies or monster films, *Born This Way* interrogated real life, which can be equally frightening. Nevertheless, Gaga was up for the challenge, as she was fired up by what she saw around her. *Born This Way* arrived at a pivotal time in American politics. Public support was growing for the legalization of same-sex marriage in the entire US, seven years after it was ruled legal in Massachusetts.

In 2011, the US military also ended its controversial "Don't Ask, Don't Tell" policy, which cleared the way for members of the LGBTQIA+ community to enlist. Gaga, who identifies as bisexual, had long been supportive of gay rights, even driving eleven hours to Maine in 2010 to speak at a rally in support of the "Don't Ask, Don't Tell" repeal. (When the ban was finally lifted, Servicemembers United in Washington, D.C.—an organization formed by veterans in support of the repeal—played her song "The Edge of Glory" at midnight in celebration.)

ABOVE With Taylor Kinney in 2014. The pair were in a relationship from 2011–2016.

Her being a member of the LGBTQIA+ community informs the power of the album's title track, which itself had roots in a classic gay anthem. "Born This Way" references a 1975 song by Valentino called "I Was Born This Way." Two years later, an artist named Carl Bean covered the song while signed to Motown Records. Bean's version was a dance hit, peaking at No. 15 on *Billboard*'s Dance Club Songs chart the following year on the strength of a funky disco backbeat and his gospel-inspired vocals.

Gaga's propulsive 2011 version builds on the empowering sentiment of the original song, and stresses that people are born unique and special. From there, she assures groups typically bullied that they are perfect just the way they are, and Gaga herself fully supports them as they embrace their individuality. She then calls out marginalized identities by name (e.g., Black people, people with disabilities, people who are gay, bi, lesbian, transgender) in a show of encouragement and solidarity. The end result is a skyscraping dancefloor filler that hit No. 1 in multiple countries and has since become a pride classic.

The song's surging vibe set the tone for *Born This Way*. "Hair" links the freedom to switch up hairstyles to the idea of malleable identity; in fact, Gaga views changing hair as a reflection of the changing self. "Judas" grapples with feeling torn between virtue and vice, in part by using biblical references to Judas being deceptive

THE ESSENTIAL... LADY GAGA

ABOVE Clarence
Clemons (L) and
Bruce Springsteen
(R) of the E Street
Band. The band's
music influenced
Born This Way,
with Clemons even
playing a sax solo
on one of the tracks.

and Jesus being betrayed three times, while "Government Hooker"
is an extended metaphor for the ways the powers that be seduce
and oppress. *Born This Way* also features plenty of empowered
anthems: "Marry the Night" encourages people to follow their
dreams, while "Highway Unicorn (Road to Love)" is her version of
the open-road dreamer anthems favored by her long-time musical
obsession, Bruce Springsteen.

Fittingly, Gaga also invoked the Boss to explain some of the
album's we're-in-this-together vibe. "[My fans] feel like they're the
underdogs that will someday be the winners," she told *Rolling Stone*.
Gaga also went right to the source—E Street Band saxophonist
Clarence Clemons—to provide a thundering sax solo on "The Edge
of Glory." Clemons even appeared in the song's video, which had
a distinct eighties vibe: Sporting a Cruella de Vil-style hairdo and
some elaborate Versace outfits, Gaga cavorts in and around a New
York City street and apartment, reclaiming the song as a way to
embrace new beginnings.

Sadly, the lyrics of this song were inspired by a different source:
the moment when she said goodbye to her paternal grandfather,

Joseph, who died on September 24, 2010. "The song's about your last moment on Earth," she said in an interview, "the moment of truth, the edge of glory is that moment right before you leave the Earth."

"The Edge of Glory" embodies *Born This Way*'s maximalist approach to music: The song has a gigantic chorus, sledgehammer rhythms, and stacks of interlocking keyboards. Gaga would characterize the album as "avant-garde techno rock" in an interview with *The Sun*. "I have sort of created a genre of metal dance techno pop music with a lot of rock anthemic choruses because that is the music that I love." She turned even more heads by then calling out the album's "really big, almost big Def Leppard-style melodies in the choruses." To emphasize this point, she worked with Robert John "Mutt" Lange—known for his meticulous, lacquered production on Def Leppard's smash records—on "Yoü And I," a song that also featured a cameo from Queen guitar god, Brian May.

Born This Way became Gaga's first chart-topper in the US, selling a staggering 1.1 million copies during its first week in stores. It helped that she appeared on *Saturday Night Live* again to promote the album, appearing with host Justin Timberlake in

ABOVE Singing while seated on a giant meat chair, Born This Way Ball tour, 2012.

OPPOSITE TOP Pictured during EuroPride 2011 in Rome, Italy.

OPPOSITE BOTTOM Performing at gay bar Nevermind, Sydney, Australia, 2011.

THE ESSENTIAL... LADY GAGA

two sketches. "The Edge of Glory" also made the Top Ten of the *Billboard* charts the week *Born This Way* hit stores.

Fashion-wise, Gaga's collaborators at the time echoed these hopeful, aspirational sentiments via outfits that challenged conventions. "At that time, there were a lot of things going on with regards to LGBTQ rights and female empowerment and all those things, and this album was really a starting point of taking back the ownership of our rights," collaborator and fashion director Nicola Formichetti told *PAPER* in 2021. "We wanted something very powerful—something strong and heroic and fearless, but with a Gaga twist."

First and foremost was the *Born This Way* cover, which found Gaga's head welded to a motorcycle, looking like a Medusa hood ornament. "I think that cover was what really set the tone for the entire era," Formichetti says, "which was about the duality of real life and fantasy, and the two worlds colliding." For the "Judas" video, designer Alex Noble crafted a fringe-draped outfit made of dark blue leather. MTV News further described the clip as "an arty reimagining of the betrayal of Jesus Christ by Judas Iscariot,"

ABOVE Lady Gaga and mom Cynthia in 2018. Together they set up the Born This Way Foundation.

with Gaga portraying Mary Magdalene, and Christ and his apostles
envisioned as a leather-clad motorcycle gang; actor Norman Reedus,
meanwhile, plays Judas.

August, meanwhile, brought the release of the "Yoü And I" video.
Directed by Laurieann Gibson and filmed in Nebraska—the state
where old flame Lüc Carl just happens to be from—the clip features
various Gaga personas, including her as a mermaid. Actor Taylor
Kinney starred in the clip—a fateful casting decision, as he and Gaga
hit it off, started dating, and later became engaged.

The cover of the "Yoü And I" single featured Gaga in drag,
in the guise of her handsome alter-ego Jo Calderone, who had
scruffy hair and sideburns and wore a white undershirt. Although
people wouldn't think twice if Gaga did something like this today,
critics back then didn't quite know what to do with Gaga's gender-
bending. For example, ABC News ran the headline, "Lady Gaga
as Jo Calderone: Brilliant or Creepy?" Jo Calderone was meant to
"manipulate the visualization of gender in as many ways as I possibly
could," Gaga told *Huffington Post*. "And in a completely different
way, sort of do that by creating what seems to be a straight man—a

THE ESSENTIAL... LADY GAGA

OPPOSITE TOP
Revving up the
crowd, during the
Born This Way Ball
Asia tour, 2012.

OPPOSITE BOTTOM
Lady Gaga as
her alter-ego Jo
Calderone with
Brian May at the
2011 MTV Video
Music Awards.

straight and quite relatable American man." On August 28, Gaga performed "Yoü And I" with guest Brian May at the 2011 MTV Video Music Awards, immersed fully in her Jo Calderone persona. In fact, the appearance started with a chain-smoking Jo giving a lengthy monologue about Gaga that felt more like a comedic roast.

In April 2012, she launched her next road trek, the Born This Way Ball. Dubbing it an "electro-metal pop-opera," she described it in a press release as "the tale of the Beginning, the genesis of the Kingdom of Fame. How we were birthed and how we will die celebrating." In practice, that translated to an elaborate, gigantic stage set dominated by a haunted gothic castle—*Us Weekly* quoted an executive noting it was the "largest scenic structure that's ever been built to tour"—narrated by Mother G.O.A.T., or a distorted Gaga head in a computer-generated geometric shape. The tour also featured fashions created for her by Versace, Armani, and Moschino ("It's been my life's dream to be dressed in Italian designers," Gaga told *Us Weekly*) and a general admission "Monster Pit" for dedicated fans.

> **"I am now a woman, I have a voice in the universe, and I want to do everything I can to become an expert in social justice."**

Unfortunately, an injury forced a premature end to the Born This Way Ball tour, in February 2013. Although initial reports noted she had a labral tear in her hip, the injury was actually much more involved and potentially career-derailing. Had she not quit the tour when she did, she might have needed a full hip replacement and been out of commission for an extended period.

Despite the enforced break, *Born This Way*'s legacy was secure. During this era, Gaga also used her newfound superstar platform to try and make the world a better place. In February 2012, Gaga and her mother, Cynthia, officially unveiled a nonprofit called the Born This Way Foundation, which today develops programs and community resources, conducts research, and provides resources to help youths succeed. "This is: I am now a woman, I have a voice in the universe, and I want to do everything I can to become an expert in social justice," Gaga stressed to the *New York Times*, "and hope I can make a difference and mobilize young people to change the world."

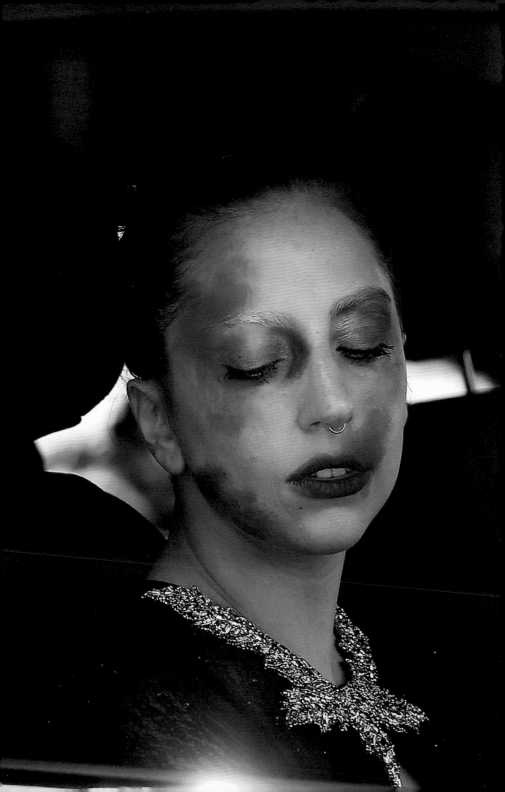

CHAPTER SEVEN

ARTPOP

Lady Gaga didn't hit a commercial stumbling block until her third album, *ARTPOP*. Although it became her second album to top the *Billboard* 200, its first-week sales numbers—258,000 copies—paled in comparison to the blockbuster, million-plus-selling *Born This Way*. Overall, *ARTPOP* only produced two hit singles, "Applause" and "Do What U Want," and polarized critics.

Part of this tepid response had to do with familiarity; lyrically, Gaga seemed to be drawing from the same themes as previous efforts. "It's my intention for you to have a really good time," Gaga told L.A. radio station KIIS-FM. "I designed it for it to be fun from start to finish, like a night at the club in terms of the DJing aspect of it." Paradoxically, pop artists had started trying to mimic Gaga's empowerment vibe and obsession with fame, but had overlooked her Warholian celebrity critiques. In other words, she had created a, well, monster: a movement of fame-obsessed pop stars who succeeded at being inspirational but didn't create music with much depth.

To be fair, Gaga herself was also trying to dial back the seriousness of her music on *ARTPOP*. The album's first single, "Applause," arrived on August 12, 2013. As with the other singles she released to preview albums, the song is bold and brash, with slamming beats, an explosive chorus, and passionate vocals. "I believe in show business," she tweeted after the song's release. "The 'Applause' is what breeds that thing that I love. When I know I've made you happy. When I know it was good." The messaging was a subtle shift from her previous songs about fame: The narrator needs that applause for validation, whereas before they might analyze the folly of craving such positive reinforcement.

The accompanying music video, directed by fashion photographer duo Inez and Vinoodh, was "inspired by the entertainer's passion for shapeshifting," Gaga tweeted. Appropriately, she switches outfits at a dizzying pace—a black full-body leotard with a head covering, a bra made from gloved hands, a green jacket comprised of what looks like tiny tiles—and references an impressive number of great works of art. The following week, Gaga opened the 2013 MTV Video Music Awards with a typically elaborate performance that ended with a big wardrobe reveal: a shell bra and bikini bottom. The outfit represented the birth of Gaga-as-Venus—and ushered in *ARTPOP*. By early September, the song peaked at No. 4 on the *Billboard* Hot 100.

On *ARTPOP*, Gaga worked with past collaborators DJ White Shadow and RedOne. However, she also teamed up with dance world A-listers—including Zedd, David Guetta, Infected Mushroom, and Madeon—enlisted Whitesnake/Dio guitarist Doug Aldrich and production whiz will.i.am, and collaborated with rappers Too $hort, Twista, and T.I. This ensured *ARTPOP*'s sound was far different from her previous efforts, even the remix albums.

ABOVE Promoting *ARTPOP* in Japan, 2013.

While nominally a mainstream dance effort with booming beats, stacked production, and Gaga's typically formidable vocals, *ARTPOP* most often feels like an underground electro-pop art project. "Swine" is industrial-metal with an EDM heart; the piano-freckled "Fashion!" has the precision and theatrical glamour of Bowie's 1980 hit; "Aura" is zippered-up robot-rock with the *savoir faire* of Daft Punk. *ARTPOP* could also have a sense of humor. The interstellar lust displayed by the narrator of "Venus" doubles as being drunk on fame, while the spelling of "MANiCURE" is deliberately meant to convey ambiguity: She pronounces the word like "man-cured," as if someone is being rescued by a guy.

The album's minimalist title track is even more intriguing. A *de facto* mission statement, it's about as confessional as Gaga gets. She admits she isn't great at being insincere or overtly self-promotional, because she's always motivated by music, not fancy things or shiny baubles. However, "Artpop" also imparts some hard-won wisdom about the importance of being resilient and staying optimistic, even (and especially) when things feel dark and hopeless. In fact, Gaga encourages people to embrace the power of music, as creativity can

THE ESSENTIAL... LADY GAGA

be a form of self-care and solace—if not personal redemption. Her vocals sometimes sound disfigured on verses, though on the chorus they're solemn and clear as a bell.

Not everything on *ARTPOP* is perfect. The overtly sexual techno-pop song "Do What U Want" featured rapper R. Kelly, who was five years removed at the time from being found not guilty on charges he filmed himself having sex with an underage girl. Years later, after the release of the documentary *Surviving R. Kelly*, which featured multiple women detailing abuse by the rapper, Gaga apologized "for my poor judgment when I was young and for not speaking out sooner" and issued a statement standing behind the brave women. She also subsequently removed "Do What U Want" from streaming services and future physical pressings of *ARTPOP*.

This situation wasn't the only hint of discord. On November 3, she made an auspicious appearance at the YouTube Music Awards. Her red-carpet look—sunglasses, a hat, and grimy prosthetic teeth—was something straight out of Tim Burton's *The Nightmare Before Christmas*. However, her performance for the new song "Dope" was worrying: Sporting a baseball hat and boxy flannel shirt, she cried at the start of the song while apologizing to her mom, and never quite recovered.

It was an auspicious sign, as critics were also hot and cold on *ARTPOP*'s music. Gaga nevertheless pressed on with elaborate promotion. She pulled double duty as host and musical guest on *Saturday Night Live*, holding her own throughout the night's skits. Looking like Donatella Versace with long, straight blonde hair and a pale purple dress, Gaga rode down the 2013 American Music Awards red carpet astride a gorgeous white "horse"—which was, in reality, two people crouched down acting like the animal. Around Thanksgiving, she did the throwback primetime variety show, *Lady Gaga & The Muppets' Holiday Spectacular*. Elton John joined Gaga on the show for a performance of his 1974 No. 1 hit "Bennie and the Jets" (which he playfully renamed to "Gaga and the Jets") and the *ARTPOP* title track.

ABOVE Riding sidesaddle on a giant white "horse" as she arrives at the 2013 American Music Awards.

However, as the *ARTPOP* campaign progressed, it became clear that behind-the-scenes professional turmoil was taking a toll—specifically, the fact that she and her long-time manager Troy Carter parted ways a week before the album came out. While some industry publications credited the split to the diplomatic (if vague) "creative differences," the *New York Times* reported that Gaga fired Carter.

Months after *ARTPOP*'s release, Gaga was clearly still processing the split with her management and how it affected the album. When asked by the *Associated Press* in September 2014 if "disagreements with management" had an impact on *ARTPOP*'s genesis, she responded, "I would have to say that whole situation had less to do with creativity differences and more to do with me really needing some time from myself to be creative."

As this conversation reveals, the *ARTPOP* era was distinguished by some of Gaga's most candid, personal interviews yet. In a December 2014 appearance on *The Howard Stern Show*, she revealed she was raped by an older producer as a "very naive"

nineteen-year-old. In fact, the song "Swine" itself is "about rape," she
added. "The song is about demoralization. The song is about rage
and fury and passion, and I had a lot of pain that I wanted to release."
Later in the interview, she noted that she didn't "want to be defined"
by the assault, and flashed her usual defiance. "I'll be damned if
somebody's gonna say that every creatively intelligent thing that I ever
did is all boiled down to one dickhead who did that to me."

She discussed her bisexuality in frank and open terms on a
separate appearance on Andy Cohen's *Watch What Happens Live*,
noting that she used to enjoy frequenting lesbian clubs ("I find
lesbians to be way more daring than straight men, when it comes to
coming on to you. And I really like that") and that "it wasn't until
I found a guy that could come on to me as strong as a lesbian"—
meaning her then-boyfriend, Taylor Kinney—"that I fell in love."

In the *ARTPOP* era, Gaga also experienced the kind of backlash
pop stars often receive—the kind that comes after sustained success—
and was forced to defend herself after making bold statements. "You
know what? It's not a lie that I am bisexual and I like women," she

said during a promotional stop. "Anyone that wants to twist this into 'she says she's bisexual for marketing,' this is a fucking lie. This is who I am and who I have always been."

As usual, Gaga's solace was a place where like-minded people gathered: her shows. In late March and early April of 2014, she played a string of concerts to send off the legendary New York City venue Roseland Ballroom. The following month, she launched artRAVE: The ARTPOP Ball. The tour's design certainly had her usual escapism vibe: In a nod to the "rave" designation, colorful lights and effects were used throughout, giving the stage a warehouse dance-party vibe. However, the show didn't neglect real-life concerns; she read heartbreaking fan mail during the show and brought people onstage to sit with her during "Born This Way."

"When I'm onstage with the ARTPOP Ball, the point of the show is to take what was the mess of my life and make art of it," she told *The Independent*. Her outfits nod to this, and included a get-up that looked like a Strawberry Shortcake character going raving; a white leotard with black polka dots and removable accents shaped into tentacles, making it appear she's being hugged by an octopus; and a silvery-white Versace dress that resembled a *Jetsons* costume. She also played some otherworldly instruments—a jaw-dropping custom keytar shaped like a seahorse and a piano nested in jagged replicas of ice shards—and sang "Paparazzi" sitting in a crystal hand with long pink nails that was bent into her "Paws up!" sign.

By the end of 2014, she was in a better headspace, making plans for future music and able to have perspective on a resurgence of depression she'd had at the end of the previous year. "Depression doesn't take away your talents—it just makes them harder to find," she told *Harper's Bazaar*. "But I always find it. I learned that my sadness never destroyed what was great about me. You just have to go back to that greatness, find that one little light that's left. I'm lucky I found one little glimmer stored away."

That glimmer ended up burning bright for years to come. After being misunderstood upon release, *ARTPOP* has become something of a cult classic, redeemed by fans and the passage of time. "I fell apart after I released this album," she tweeted in 2021. "Thank you for celebrating something that once felt like destruction. We always believed it was ahead of its time. Years later turns out, sometimes, artists know. And so do little monsters. Paws up."

PAGE 92–93 Posing "Paws up!" with her dancers, 2014.

OPPOSITE Lady Gaga brings artRAVE: The ARTPOP Ball tour to Madison Square Garden, 2014.

THE ESSENTIAL... LADY GAGA

CHAPTER EIGHT

CHEEK TO CHEEK

PAGE 96 Playing piano at a benefit gala in New York, 2011: a performance that wowed Tony Bennett.

OPPOSITE Lady Gaga and Tony Bennett perform live onstage at The Wiltern, in Los Angeles, California, 2015.

On paper, Lady Gaga and Tony Bennett didn't seem to have much in common. He was a senior citizen jazz crooner; she was a metal-loving pop singer millennial. However, both artists were incredibly versatile—Bennett had massive pop success decades before Gaga was born, including with 1962's "I Left My Heart in San Francisco"—and both were prone to reinvention. For example, Bennett was also a decorated painter, and he performed on *MTV Unplugged* in the nineties with artists such as Elvis Costello and k.d. lang. Still, Gaga's pivot from scrappy performance artist to sophisticated jazz chanteuse is one of music's great unexpected evolutions. That her collaborations with Bennett worked so well— and sounded so natural—is also a marvel.

The pair first crossed paths in 2011 at a Robin Hood Foundation benefit gala where Gaga performed. Bennett was particularly wowed by the pop star's take on Nat King Cole's "Orange Colored Sky" and asked to meet her. He gauged her interest in doing a jazz album together—her answer was a quick yes—and their friendship began. Gaga became so fond of him, in fact, she got a tattoo of a Bennett sketch of a trumpet in June 2014.

The proposed full-length album took some time to coalesce, as Gaga was laid up recovering from her *Born This Way* tour injuries. However, the pair knew their collaboration was going to work, as they tracked a peppy, playful take on Rodgers and Hart's "The Lady Is a Tramp" for Bennett's 2011 album, *Duets II*. The crooner couldn't say enough good things about Gaga at the time, praising her singing, dancing, and piano skills. "She's as good as Ella Fitzgerald or anybody you want to come up with," Bennett told

CHAPTER EIGHT CHEEK TO CHEEK

Rolling Stone. "I know it sounds way out, but she could become America's Picasso if they leave her alone and let her just do what she has to do."

Three years later, when Gaga and Bennett taped a concert for the PBS show *Great Performances*, he echoed these sentiments. Walking the red carpet before the show, which took place at the Rose Theater of Jazz at Lincoln Center, Bennett stressed to *Rolling Stone* that it wasn't *what* Gaga sang but *how* she sang it that stood out. "She phrases like I phrase," he said. "She's a wonderful singer... I think when they hear this album that we're doing, they're going to say, 'We had no idea that she sings that well.'"

Part of this change in style had to do with the supportive, hospitable recording environment Bennett fostered. "On my earlier records they wanted to make my voice more electronic and auto-tuned for radio," Gaga told *Parade*. "That's why this album with Tony is so amazing, because he's hearing me sing raw, without any of that. And he's protecting me from people trying to control what I sound like." On *Cheek to Cheek*, Gaga sounds completely different than she does on her pop records; her croon is rich and luxurious, like crushed velvet, and she has the space to explore greater emotional range.

When the pair convened to record *Cheek to Cheek*, they also went all out instrumentally, hiring dozens of jazz musicians to bring their performances to life. Both Gaga and Bennett invoked Amy Winehouse when discussing the album's inspiration. "I thought of her almost every day in the studio," Gaga said during a Twitter Q&A. "I wish she was still here. She was jazz to her core." Bennett added, "I'm sure that she would be proud and that makes me feel good."

Like Winehouse's *Back to Black*, which put an updated spin on retro sounds, the duo's collaborative take on the standards was

THE ESSENTIAL... LADY GAGA

both fresh and classic. Upbeat songs such as "Goody Goody" and "It Don't Mean a Thing (If It Ain't Got That Swing)" boasted impeccable vocal precision, while Gaga's solo take on Cole Porter's "Ev'ry Time We Say Goodbye" is sweetly sad.

Gaga also gravitated toward Billy Strayhorn's "Lush Life," a song she recalled singing as a teenager. "I didn't understand what the lyrics were about, but I understood the melody in a very intense way," she told *Parade*. "Now I know everything that song is about. When I sang it [on this album] for the first time in 15 years, I started crying." Her performance of "Lush Life" on *Cheek to Cheek* is stunning and sophisticated; it's clear she relates especially deeply to the lyrics about loneliness.

Her long-time friends—like her Lower East Side co-conspirator, Lady Starlight—were blown away by her turn to jazz. "It just didn't sound like her singing; the quality of the voice, the phrasing, everything, it was so interesting," she told *Rolling Stone*. "For me to hear her sing pop and rock ballads, it made me understand more about her. I could hear how she changed her voice."

ABOVE (L-R) Tony Bennett, Lady Gaga, Cynthia and husband Joe Germanotta at the live recording of *Cheek to Cheek*.

ABOVE Julie
Andrews embraces
Lady Gaga
following Gaga's
Sound of Music
tribute at the 2015
Academy Awards.

Cheek to Cheek debuted at No. 1 on the US *Billboard* 200 album charts, selling 131,000 copies during its first week on sale, and also charted well in the UK, Australia, Canada, Greece, Italy, and Japan. It was Gaga's third chart-topping album to date, and helped Bennett set a rather impressive career record: At eighty-eight, he was the oldest artist to land a No. 1 album on the charts. *Cheek to Cheek* also won a Grammy Award for Best Traditional Pop Vocal Album. The concert they taped, *Tony Bennett & Lady Gaga: Cheek to Cheek Live!*, debuted on PBS in October.

Soon after, she and Bennett launched their *Cheek to Cheek* tour, playing festivals and also performing "Cheek to Cheek" at the Grammy Awards. Their onstage chemistry mirrored what was heard on the album; in fact, they brought out the best in each other.

In February 2015, Gaga took a brief break from her work with Bennett to attend the Oscars and perform a heartfelt tribute to another great songbook: music from 1965's *The Sound of Music*. She was nervous about getting the songs right—so much so that she called the film's star, Julie Andrews. The actress was impressed by Gaga's work ethic. "She said she'd been working so hard and she was singing everything in my keys. I said, 'Why? They're very high, even for me.' And she said, 'Because I wanted to honor you, so I did them in your keys.' That seemed like going one step beyond any place she needed to go." The hard work certainly paid off: Gaga sounded stunning, nailing the songs without breaking a sweat.

She and Bennett reconvened and kept touring through August 2015. And then, a year later, Gaga performed at an event for Bennett's ninetieth birthday party, where she sang "Happy Birthday to You," dueted with Stevie Wonder on "Signed, Sealed, Delivered (I'm Yours)," and unfurled a sultry, jazzy version of "Bad Romance" on solo piano.

Other performers might have ended their pairing there; however, Gaga's loyalty and affection for the legend were too strong to dissipate. "Tony told me Frank Sinatra changed his life when he said 'For my money, Tony Bennett is the best singer in the business,'" Gaga wrote in a Twitter Q&A. "Tony is MY Frank. What he has done for me will change my career forever. And I truly cherish our friendship." Gaga kept her word: She and Bennett recorded a follow-up to *Cheek to Cheek* between 2018 and 2020, a period during which Bennett became increasingly affected by Alzheimer's disease.

In an *AARP* article revealing the crooner's diagnosis, Gaga is described as an empathetic and tender collaborator who altered her speech patterns specifically to communicate better with Bennett as they spent time together. Her gratitude for his unconditional support—and being able to reciprocate the support he initially gave to her—was even more palpable: "The fact that Tony sees me as a natural-born jazz singer is still something that I haven't gotten over."

In July 2021, Gaga and Bennett announced two shows at Radio City Music Hall to celebrate Bennett's ninety-fifth birthday and film a TV special. These shows came with official news of the new

ABOVE Lady Gaga shows off her trumpet tattoo designed by Tony Bennett.

THE ESSENTIAL... LADY GAGA

ABOVE Gaga sings
to Bennett at his
ninetieth birthday
celebrations, 2016.

PAGE 106–107
At the 57th Annual
Grammy Awards
in 2015.

album, *Love for Sale*, a collection of Cole Porter covers introduced by a sizzling take on "I Get a Kick Out of You." In a glowing review of the first Radio City Music Hall show, *USA Today* noted the pair dueted together on three of their signature songs: "The Lady Is a Tramp," "Anything Goes," and "It Don't Mean a Thing (If It Ain't Got That Swing)." Bennett was also "as spry and charismatic as ever" during a half-hour solo set that included multiple standing ovations.

Sadly, Bennett died on July 21, 2023. Gaga's Instagram message in his honor was honest and heartbroken. "With Tony, I got to live my life in a time warp," she wrote. "Tony and I had this magical power. We transported ourselves to another era, modernized the music together, and gave it all new life as a singing duo. But it wasn't an act. Our relationship was very real." One might think that Bennett received more of a boost from working with a younger artist like Gaga. However, it's clear that working with Bennett saved Gaga—and righted the ship of her career.

CHAPTER NINE

JOANNE

PAGE 108
Headlining the
Super Bowl LI
Halftime show,
2017.

OPPOSITE Lady
Gaga leans on her
disco stick during
her *Joanne* World
Tour, 2017.

When Lady Gaga turned her focus back to pop-oriented music after doing *Cheek to Cheek* with Tony Bennett, she teamed up with one of the most successful songwriters in the world, Diane Warren, for the stunning "Til It Happens to You," which was heard in *The Hunting Ground*, a documentary about sexual assault on college campuses.

The song paired several Warren hallmarks, including sweeping dynamics and orchestral flourishes, with an understated Gaga vocal performance brimming with empathy. The latter made sure the song didn't come across as downtrodden or defeated, but featured a narrator that wasn't going to let the assault undermine her strength. As Gaga put it: "[The song] became two women together, standing strong."

"Til It Happens to You" won a Primetime Emmy Award for Outstanding Original Music and Lyrics, and it was nominated for a Grammy Award for Best Song Written for Visual Media and an Academy Award for Best Original Song. Gaga's 2016 Oscars performance was deeply moving: She wore a simple white suit and played an all-white piano onstage by herself before introducing fifty other survivors of assault—a gesture that signified people don't have to go through traumatic experiences by themselves.

While promoting "Til It Happens to You," Gaga started opening up about her own rape, telling the *Hollywood Reporter*'s *Awards Chatter* podcast that she was assaulted by someone she knew ("It was done to manipulate me in conjunction with money and my music, and it was terrifying") and that the attack still had a profound impact. "It's something that changed me forever, and it made me question everything about what I had done to be where I am today."

The topics brought up in "Til It Happens to You" also had deep meaning to her family. Her father's sister, Joanne Germanotta, was sexually assaulted in college, Gaga revealed at the 2015 Producers Guild of America Awards. "Then, it tormented her so emotionally that it caused the lupus that she had to get so bad that she died."

Joanne Germanotta looms large in Gaga's universe. Born in 1955, she was just nineteen when she died on December 18, 1974. Her death understandably had a profound impact on her family, Gaga told *The Sunday Times*. "My whole life, I never understood why my father was so sad, drank so much or was wild. I thought it was my fault, and it was painful for the family. I'd witness year after year that feeling of loss within my father and grandparents."

Even though Gaga was not yet born when Joanne passed away, her late aunt has always been something of a benevolent guiding presence. Her middle name is Joanne, and she has her aunt's signature and date of death tattooed on her arm, the latter right near text from Rainer Maria Rilke's *Letters to a Young Poet*. And, over the years, she mentioned Joanne consistently in interviews— culminating in a decision to title her fifth studio album, *Joanne*.

The emotion behind this choice is on display in the 2017 Netflix documentary *Gaga: Five Foot Two*, which covers the making of *Joanne*. In one of the documentary's most affecting moments, Gaga visits her grandmother and reminisces while going through family photographs and old papers, including some of Joanne's writing. "She had a lot of talent but she didn't have enough time," her grandmother says of her beloved daughter, before Gaga plays her the title track via her iPhone. The sadness within the song is palpable even through the tiny speaker; Gaga's father, who's also with them listening, is overcome with emotion and has to leave the room.

ABOVE With songwriter Diane Warren.

OPPOSITE TOP LEFT Joe and Cynthia Germanotta with Gaga's grandmother.

OPPOSITE TOP RIGHT The *Joanne* era, 2016.

OPPOSITE BOTTOM The Joanne Trattoria restaurant owned by Gaga's parents on the Upper West Side, New York.

THE ESSENTIAL... LADY GAGA

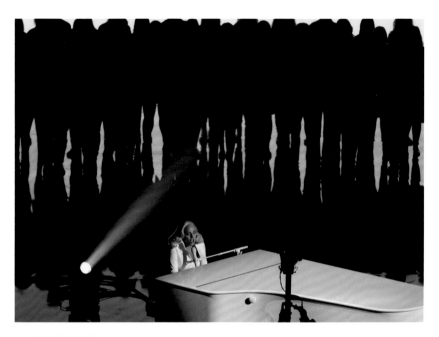

THE ESSENTIAL... LADY GAGA

"That's beautiful," Gaga's grandmother says several times after the song finishes, as the pop star starts crying. "You're just so special." The two then embrace.

Seeing the photos brought Joanne to life, and made it clearer why the woman means so much to Gaga. Speaking to the *New York Times*, Gaga noted that she herself was nineteen—the age Joanne was when she passed—when her musical life began. "I used to leave my apartment and I just had my white boots on and my little shorts and a T-shirt and I would just walk down the street on the Lower East Side totally free. And I had the whole world— the whole unknown of music—and where it could take me ahead of me."

The title track she played for her grandmother is especially meaningful, she added. "And this song ['Joanne'] in a

OPPOSITE TOP A moving performance at the 2016 Academy Awards.

OPPOSITE BOTTOM The Joanne World Tour comes to Little Caesars Arena, Detroit, Michigan, 2017.

ABOVE A new low-key look for Lady Gaga.

lot of ways I realized even today is me looking back on Joanne and saying 'Where do you think you're going?' You know, I had no idea where I was going." Driven by unadorned acoustic guitar, simple pitter-patter drums, and subtle orchestra swells, "Joanne" is indeed a moving farewell to her aunt. At first, the heartfelt song is grief-stricken, although later on, she is comforted by thoughts of eternal love and the idea that her aunt is thriving in an afterlife as an angel.

Musically, *Joanne* felt like a sonic departure for Gaga. Tame Impala's Kevin Parker co-wrote and co-produced "Perfect Illusion," ensuring the song's pulsing electro-pop had a lighter touch than previous Gaga dancefloor bangers, while noted country-pop songwriter Hillary Lindsey co-wrote "Million Reasons." Elsewhere, *Joanne* references Motown and country (the harmony-heavy "Come to Mama"), punkish twang ("A-YO"), and seventies confessional pop (the warm "Just Another Day").

Working with producer Mark Ronson also pushed her songwriting into even deeper personal territory. This led to "Grigio Girls," a touching song about her friend Sonja Durham and her journey living with cancer, and "Angel Down," a song inspired

ABOVE Performing a David Bowie tribute with Nile Rodgers at the 2016 Grammy Awards.

by the murder of teenager Trayvon Martin. "Perfect Illusion," meanwhile, is a breakup song that doubles as a song about the perils of idolatry, while Gaga said "Diamond Heart" is a "completely autobiographical" song about maintaining inner self-confidence (her "diamond heart") despite the odds. "Life is a dog fight for a lot of people," she told *NME*. "When you find the pitbull within yourself, that's Joanne."

Joanne also featured a bevy of interesting (and even unexpected) guest collaborators. Queens of the Stone Age's Josh Homme added humid guitar scorch to "Diamond Heart," while Gaga duets with Florence Welch of Florence and the Machine on "Hey Girl," a dewy, funky slow jam about the power of friendship. Her collaboration with Beck is an equally funky song, "Dancin' in Circles," that grew out of an impromptu, low-key studio jam.

Some of these names might be surprising to those who only know Gaga's pop side. However, this open-mindedness was a hallmark of *Joanne*. "I love a sugary sweet sound that has a message underneath it, or perhaps something darker or different," she told *Entertainment Weekly*. "*Joanne* is not dark in the way that *The Fame Monster* was,

but it's dark in a different way. Not darkness as horror—it's dark in the way that things can life be dark."

The cover of *Joanne* was markedly tamer: It featured a very simple photograph of Gaga in profile, sporting a petal-pink velour cowboy hat made by the L.A.-based milliner Gladys Tamez. According to Tamez, the hat served as something like a muse for Gaga during the *Joanne* era. "She put the hat on and got in the bathtub and started writing the record," she told *The Daily Beast*. "It represents more of who she is inside as opposed to her public persona. The hat is central in a symbolic sense to who this new Lady Gaga is."

Joanne debuted at No. 1 on the *Billboard* album charts and was nominated for a Grammy for Best Pop Vocal Album, while "Million Reasons" earned a nod for Best Pop Solo Performance. Perhaps even more important, the album's title track also had a profound impact on Gaga's dad. "I saw a look in my dad's eyes that I've never seen in my whole life," she told the audience during an October 2016 performance at The Satellite in Los Angeles. "Sometimes I used to wonder if I ever got to meet my real dad, you know, because sometimes things happen in your life that are so bad that you die, or a part of you dies." *Joanne*, however, was restorative. "After this record came out, I swear that part of my dad came back to life. I hope that when you hear it when you're with your families and you think of the loss that you've had or the pending loss... I hope this song can heal you like it healed my family."

Many elements of the *Joanne* era nodded to her past. At the 2016 Grammy Awards, she teamed up with Nile Rodgers—with whom she had covered Chic's "I Want Your Love" to promote designer Tom Ford's spring/summer collection—and paid tribute to David Bowie with a stirring medley. That same month, Gaga sang the US national anthem at Super Bowl 50, nailing the high notes with

"Life is a dog fight for a lot of people. When you find the pitbull within yourself, that's Joanne."

confidence while sporting a metallic red suit. Later in 2016, she did a three-city Dive Bar Tour, which gave her the chance to perform on the roof of her old stomping ground, The Bitter End, as crowds of people swarmed below on the street and cheered her on.

On February 5, 2017, she reached another career milestone as she headlined the Super Bowl LI halftime show at NRG Stadium in Houston, Texas. Unlike other Super Bowl halftime shows, Gaga didn't have any high-profile special guests or flashy celebrity cameos. Instead, the entire show focused on her and her formidable catalog of hits.

In August, Gaga launched the Joanne World Tour. Although there were no shortage of costume changes and elaborate moments—including trippy interstitial videos that depicted (among other things) her having a rhino horn on her forehead and a baggy, bright-red dress for "Bloody Mary"—her outfits and the stage decor were more in line with *Joanne*'s understated vibe. For "A-YO," she strapped on a sparkly guitar and did a little country line dance to the twangy song; "LoveGame" brought a cowboy-sweetheart pale-blue-denim bodysuit with pearl accents and matching boots; and for "Born This Way," she wore a fluffy white tulle skirt and fresh floral-print jacket. However, other parts of the show connected to her past: She hauled around a custom keytar with fringes for "Just Dance," and at other times wielded a gigantic disco stick with a sharp-edged, geometric star on top.

The tour wrapped ten shows early (due to fibromyalgia; in 2017, she had revealed that she lived with the painful condition). In hindsight, being so personal on *Joanne* was "really hard," she told the *Associated Press*. "But it was the best thing I ever did going there, because once you go there, you can't get darker than there 'cause you just got to look inside and whatever it is it is, and then you pick yourself up and keep going."

THE ESSENTIAL... LADY GAGA

CHAPTER TEN

A FILM STAR IS BORN

PAGE 120 Lady
Gaga poses with
her Oscar for Best
Original Song, 2019.

OPPOSITE At the
premiere of *A Star
Is Born*, Venice Film
Festival, 2018.

In the documentary *Gaga: Five Foot Two*, Lady Gaga talked about losing the loves of her life as she became more successful and her career took off; most recently, she and Taylor Kinney cancelled their engagement in 2016, after she signed up for *A Star Is Born*. Gaga also continued to deal with multiple physical health problems, most notably fibromyalgia, a disorder marked by chronic pain in places such as muscles and joints. *Gaga: Five Foot Two* shows her on a couch in anguish, and also at the doctor seeking relief. "Chronic pain is no joke," she told *Vogue*. "And it's every day waking up not knowing how you're going to feel."

Despite this discord, Gaga was on the verge of fulfilling one childhood dream: becoming a big-time actress, starring opposite Bradley Cooper in his directorial debut, a modern take on *A Star Is Born*. Originating as a Technicolor movie in 1937, it was remade as a musical in 1954 with Judy Garland and James Mason before, most famously, Kris Kristofferson and Barbra Streisand starred in the 1976 remake that won the Academy Award for Best Original Song at 1977's Oscars for the theme song, "Evergreen."

Cooper decided to hire Gaga as his co-star after catching her performing at a backyard cancer benefit. "She had her hair slicked back, and she sang 'La Vie en rose,' and I was just... levitating," he recalled to *Vogue*. "It shot like a diamond through my brain. I loved the way she moved, the sound of her voice." The very next day, he drove to Malibu—and Gaga had a similar jolt of recognition and familiarity. "The second that I saw him, I was like, 'Have I known you my whole life?'" she told *Vogue*. "It was an instant connection, instant understanding of one another."

Over a lunch of spaghetti and meatballs, the pair started talking and then ended up performing the traditional folk song "Midnight Special." Gaga, who was on piano, was blown away by Cooper's voice. "He sings from his gut, from the nectar!" she told *Vogue*. "I knew instantly: This guy could play a rock star." Gaga had the foresight to film their duet on her phone; Cooper showed the video to Warner Bros., which helped the movie move forward into production.

By the time *A Star Is Born* started filming, Gaga had plenty of professional acting experience and voiceover work under her belt. There were her holiday variety shows, of course, but also a 2012 voiceover appearance on *The Simpsons*, where she was tasked with elevating the mood of Lisa Simpson and the rest of Springfield. She also appeared in two Robert Rodriguez films, 2013's *Machete Kills* and 2014's *Sin City: A Dame to Kill For*.

In late 2015, she started portraying her biggest role yet: the murder-loving Countess in *American Horror Story: Hotel*. Gaga called playing this role "a dream come true," and approached the Countess role with her usual intensity, drawing on her years studying

ABOVE French movie posters for *Sin City: A Dame to Kill For*, 2014, and *Machete Kills*, 2013 (R).

THE ESSENTIAL... LADY GAGA

method acting to become fully absorbed in her character. "I become
The Countess in the car on my way to work," she continued. "I put
fishnet on my face and red lipstick on and I read my lines. I am
always prepared before I come to the trailer."

Her dedication to the craft paid off: On January 10, 2016, she
won a Golden Globe for Best Performance by an Actress in a TV
Movie or Miniseries for the role. She followed up the award-winning
part by returning to the series in fall 2016, where she portrayed a
witch named Scáthach, in *American Horror Story: Roanoke.* In
contrast to The Countess, Scáthach was grittier and scarier, with a
matted, red-brown wig and dirty makeup.

A Star Is Born started production in April 2017 at Coachella,
specifically during the week of downtime between both weekends
of the festival. (Gaga happened to be headlining the real thing.)
For authenticity, they continued to film at actual music festival
sites, including the country-leaning Stagecoach—a scene shot in
eight minutes "between Jamey Johnson and Willie Nelson," Cooper
recalled—and in front of a packed crowd of 80,000 people at
Glastonbury in England.

The latter was something of a full-circle moment: Kris Kristofferson, co-star of the award-winning 1976 musical version of *A Star Is Born* himself, let Cooper share the stage. "[He] was kind enough to give us four minutes of his set," the actor revealed. "I sang, played the guitar solo, and then I said, 'Ladies and gentlemen, Kris Kristofferson.'"

Gaga found some other parallels to her career in the script, such as when Cooper (as Jackson Maine) finishes a performance and comes offstage to dead silence. "This is how I feel as a performer," she explained to *Elle*. "That's what it feels like when you go onstage and there are 20,000 people screaming... and then the show is over and there's no sound. It's emotional."

OPPOSITE TOP
Lady Gaga plays witch Scáthach in *American Horror Story: Roanoke*.

OPPOSITE BOTTOM
(L-R) Anthony Rossomando, Andrew Wyatt, Lady Gaga, and Mark Ronson pose with their award for Best Original Song at the Golden Globes, 2019.

"That's what it feels like when you go onstage and there are 20,000 people screaming ... and then the show is over and there's no sound. It's emotional."

But while it might be easy to say she and her character in the movie were one and the same, that's far from the case. While Gaga clearly drew on her upbringing and early days in music for *A Star Is Born*, it was no biopic. Although many musicians are self-conscious when they switch to movies—or end up portraying thinly veiled versions of their real selves—Gaga disappeared fully into the role of Ally, an aspiring singer who's thrust into the spotlight after a chance encounter with troubled rock star Jackson Maine.

Early on, when she wows the crowd at a drag bar by singing "La Vie en rose," she dials back any Gaga-isms and channels her more theatrical side. Ally's overall approach to pop is also more muted and conventional than Lady Gaga's—and Gaga pulls it off. "The character of Ally is informed by my life experience," she told *Elle*. "But I also wanted to make sure that she was not me. It was a cadence of both."

Gaga did admit a deep kinship to her character. "I feel Ally inside of me," she told *Variety* in fall 2018. "I wonder how long she'll stay. Or if she'll be in there forever." In fact, Gaga snuck in to see the movie during its theatrical run, but had to leave before the film ended because she was so overcome with emotion.

A Star Is Born earned $215.3 million overall at the box office in the US and Canada. In addition to this success, the film also had a hit soundtrack that topped the charts around the world, including in the US, UK, and Canada. Produced in part by country whiz Dave Cobb, the release featured a mix of covers and original songwriting contributions from Gaga and some of Nashville's finest songwriters: Jason Isbell, Natalie Hemby, Hillary Lindsey, Lori McKenna, and Lukas Nelson. Appropriately, the album is full of rugged Americana and country rock, spliced with doses of seventies classic rock and folk.

Together, Gaga and Cooper also had a major crossover pop smash with the searing duet "Shallow." Co-written by Gaga, Mark Ronson, Anthony Rossomando, and Andrew Wyatt, the song (rightfully) dominated the 2019 awards show season. A conversation between two people who aren't quite connecting, "Shallow" is about being over your head in a relationship, teetering on the edge of drowning but trying to find a solution to make things work. Near the middle of the song, Gaga goes to her higher range and bellows lyrics about jumping into a bottomless deep end, which propels the song to soaring emotional heights. The anguish she feels because of her partner sears like a brand.

A Star Is Born itself also received dozens of award nominations, including multiple individual acting nods for Gaga and Cooper. At the Golden Globe Awards in early January, Gaga lost the Best Performance in a Motion Picture – Drama award to Glenn Close but won Best Original Song for "Shallow." She looked fantastic nonetheless, sporting a strapless, baby-blue Valentino couture dress with billowing sleeves, and a simple topknot dyed the same color as the frock.

A few weeks later, when the Oscar nominations were announced, any disappointment dissipated: She was nominated for the coveted Best Actress and Best Original Song awards. Incredibly enough, she was only the second person ever to receive nominations for both acting and songwriting for the same film in a given year; only Mary J. Blige had achieved this feat previously, for 2017's *Mudbound*.

Cooper and Gaga blurred fantasy and reality for their performance of "Shallow" at the Oscars. As a guitarist played the song's heart-stirring acoustic riff offscreen, the couple walked up to the stage from the front row, hand-in-hand. Cooper sang the first

verse directly to Gaga, who stood still before sitting down at the piano and taking the lead. Her voice grew in passion and intensity until the song's electric ending, which culminated with Cooper joining her on the piano bench to end the performance singing together at one mic. The intimate duet captured the delicacy and turbulence of their characters' onscreen relationship.

Unsurprisingly, "Shallow" took home the Academy Award for Best Original Song. A tearful Gaga, wearing a halter-neckline black Brandon Maxwell dress, thanked her family and co-writers, before saving perhaps her biggest compliment for Cooper: "Thank you for believing in us." She again lost the acting award, this time to Olivia Colman, but picked up two more awards for "Shallow" at the Grammys that February. Her performance of the song there hewed toward devilish glam: She fronted a sleek electric rock band while sporting a jewel-bedecked catsuit and Bowie-caliber high boots. When all was said and done, Gaga became the first woman ever to win an Oscar, Grammy, Golden Globe, and BAFTA in the same year. For good measure, during the week of March 9, "Shallow" hit No. 1 on the *Billboard* Hot 100 singles chart.

Despite any losses, Gaga's acting career—and the *A Star Is Born* soundtrack—had incredible momentum. In 2021, she starred as the lead in *House of Gucci*, Ridley Scott's long-gestating biopic on the Gucci family. She portrayed Patrizia Reggiani, or Lady Gucci, who has a sordid past: she was tried and convicted of orchestrating the assassination of her ex-husband, family patriarch Maurizio Gucci. Couture luxe fashion and dramatic Italian family stories—Gaga was tailor-made for the role. She drew raves for her performance, with one critic calling it "Oscar-worthy" and another reviewer saying she was "never less than fascinating to watch." Among other things, she received a Screen Actors Guild Awards nomination for Outstanding Performance by a Female Actor in a Leading Role.

ABOVE Lady Gaga as Patrizia Reggiani on the set of *House of Gucci.*

P130–131 Bradley Cooper and Lady Gaga perform "Shallow" at the 2019 Academy Awards.

CHAPTER ELEVEN

CHROMATICA

Years ago, Las Vegas residencies were reserved for veteran artists considered washed-up or in the twilight of their careers. However, thanks to the blockbuster residencies booked by acts such as Celine Dion and Kylie Minogue, as well as the proliferation of mega-dance clubs anchored by superstar DJs, current-day Vegas is a cool, in-demand musical locale.

In late December 2018, Lady Gaga made a splash in Vegas with a high-profile residency. The concert skillfully nodded to Sin City's split personality: One version of the show was an over-the-top pop extravaganza called Enigma, while another one was a classy, old-fashioned revue dubbed Jazz & Piano. Gaga is the rare modern pop star who can pull off both musical styles equally well, meaning either concert was a satisfying watch.

According to a *Rolling Stone* review, the pop show was narrated by an "alien guardian angel" who warned that Gaga can only move forward in life if she revisits and embraces the past. (Call it a cutting-edge, modern version of *A Christmas Carol*.) Jazz & Piano, meanwhile, highlighted the more grown-up, straitlaced music she favored on albums like *Cheek to Cheek*. Enigma was a roaring success, grossing $53.87 million in 2019 and pushing Gaga over the $500 million mark for career touring earnings, making her only the fifth woman to achieve this milestone. The residency was due to restart in spring 2020, until the COVID-19 pandemic forced the show to go dark, picking up again in late 2021 and continuing through to summer 2024.

In 2020, Gaga revealed something else brewing: *Chromatica*, her sixth studio album and first straight-up pop effort since 2013's

ARTPOP. If the album title also sounds kind of like the name of a glittery distant planet, you'd be correct. "I found Earth, I deleted it," she said in a radio interview promoting the LP. "Earth is cancelled. I live on Chromatica." The planet, naturally, was welcoming to all.

To beam listeners to *Chromatica*, she teamed up with some familiar names (producer BloodPop and musician Madeon, her old pals Justin Tranter, Elton John, Max Martin) and a bevy of cutting-edge electro collaborators, including SOPHIE, Swedish House Mafia's Axwell, Boys Noize, Morgan Kibby, and Skrillex. "It felt right for her to revisit electronic elements, so we came straight out of the gates with pulsating synths and house rhythms," BloodPop told *Entertainment Weekly*, noting that the "Enigma" demo kickstarted the album's direction. "It felt like a mix of Studio 54 and threads of all our favorite dance records. It evoked that fleeting, euphoric feeling that comes from good dance music."

Indeed, *Chromatica* has a distinctly throwback vibe that touches on glittery seventies disco, kicky eighties new wave, and triumphant nineties house music. "We weren't going for modern EDM, we were going for classic-feeling dance music," producer BURNS

THE ESSENTIAL... LADY GAGA

told *Entertainment Weekly*. "'Authentic' was a word I used a lot;
it had to be familiar, but also fresh at the same time." To that end,
"Alice" boasts a Korg M1 organ bass, while BURNS added, "I was
conscious of trying to steer away from that polished, crisp sound you
hear in a lot of current pop-EDM production. I wanted everything I
was a part of to have character and a bit of grit to it."

That same vibe extended to the album's videos. "Rain on Me"
featured Ariana Grande, Gaga, and a bevy of dancers celebrating
in a dark (and, yes, damp) post-apocalyptic scene, while looking like
cutting-edge club kids. The iPhone-shot video for "Stupid Love,"
meanwhile, showed the lighter side of the end-of-the-world dance
club. Seemingly set on Planet Chromatica, Gaga leads a gang of
pink-clad revelers while wearing a risqué outfit: satin bra, underwear
studded with spikes, a high ponytail and long hair extensions, and a
heart-shaped forehead charm. In a nod to the song's positive vibe,
Gaga uses telekinesis to separate two dancers who start sparring. The
message is clear: Choose love and unity, not violence.

The uplift was at odds with the album's rollout: *Chromatica*'s
release was initially delayed due to the COVID-19 pandemic, which

began to surge just as promotion started. In an interview, Gaga also opened up to Oprah Winfrey about the sexual assault she had first started talking about in 2014. Much had changed in the past six years: The #MeToo movement rippling through the entertainment industry inspired celebrities in multiple industries to come forward about their experiences, while conversations about mental health were more common and encouraged. Gaga was more honest than she had ever been, revealing she became pregnant from the assault and had a "total psychotic break" afterward that brought on a diagnosis of PTSD. "For a couple years, I was not the same girl."

This wasn't the only trauma she revisited. In an Apple Music interview, she confessed to host Zane Lowe that she thought she fell short with one of the aims of *Joanne*: easing the pain her dad felt from his sister's death. This particular admission contradicted what she had said in the wake of *Joanne*'s release—that her dad had felt some relief—which made her statement much sadder.

Writing and recording *Chromatica* itself also brought up some difficult emotions that weighed heavily on her. "I used to wake up in the morning, and I would realize I was 'Lady Gaga.' And then I

ABOVE Lady Gaga chats with Oprah on Oprah's 2020 Vision: Your Life in Focus tour.

THE ESSENTIAL... LADY GAGA

ABOVE Showcasing Enigma, a pop extravaganza, at Park Theater, Las Vegas, 2018.

became very depressed and sad, and I didn't want to be myself," she told *People*. "I felt threatened by the things my career brought into my life and the pace of my life." This heavy mood affected her creativity, she added. "I spent a lot of time in a sort of catatonic state of just not wanting to do anything. And then I finally, slowly started to make music and tell my story through my record."

Understandably, *Chromatica* boasts some of the most vulnerable lyrics of her career. The first non-instrumental song, "Alice" (as in Wonderland), captured uncertainty, while "Replay" is about the claustrophobic and painful experience of being forced to re-live past traumas. Another *Chromatica* highlight, "911," references an antipsychotic medication called olanzapine, which she takes "because I can't always control things that my brain does," she told Apple Music.

Appropriately, the song's surreal, brightly colored video—directed by filmmaker Tarsem Singh, who won an MTV Video Music Award for R.E.M.'s "Losing My Religion" but hadn't directed a music video in over twenty years—reflects the spatial and mental disorientation that might occur without this pharmaceutical

THE ESSENTIAL... LADY GAGA

"The beginning of the album really symbolizes, for me, what I would call the beginning of my journey to healing."

help. On Instagram, she wrote that the video covers "the way reality and dreams can interconnect to form heroes within us and all around us," and thanked her fans for their support.

The realization that she can move forward from trauma turned out to be one of *Chromatica*'s most poignant themes. The sentiment of "Rain on Me" is that she'd rather be open about her life, warts and all, than keep it hidden. And "Free Woman" especially was her way of reclaiming her truth due to her assault. "I tend to aspire for things to be genderless," she told Apple Music. "[But] I felt a need to reference my gender because I was assaulted by a music producer." She added, "I no longer am going to define myself as a survivor or a victim of sexual assault. I just am a person that is free who went through some fucked-up shit."

That strength resonated with fans, as *Chromatica* debuted at No. 1 in the US and UK, and also topped the charts in Austria, Italy, New Zealand, Portugal, and Switzerland, among other countries. "That the beginning of the album really symbolizes, for me, what I would call the beginning of my journey to healing," Gaga told Apple Music, "and what I would hope would be an inspiration for people that are in need of healing through happiness, through dance."

Perhaps even more important, Gaga added that she forgave herself "for all the ways I've punished myself in private," such as cutting herself. "I've been open about the fact that I have had masochistic tendencies that are not healthy. They're ways of expressing shame. They're ways of expressing feeling not good enough. But actually, they're not effective. They just make you feel worse."

However, not everything about the *Chromatica* era was painful. For example, fans could buy limited edition Gaga-themed Oreos of pale pink cookies and sea-foam green filling. And, despite challenges related to social distancing and the pandemic lockdown, Gaga brought nine different looks to the 2020 MTV Video Music Awards.

Her red carpet fashion choice was astronaut chic: She paired a clear bubble helmet and black platform boots with a flowing dress made out of silver material, making her appear swaddled in aluminum foil.

Later, she donned a series of elaborate face masks—including a robotic one that featured red and white sine waves in time with her singing voice—and performed "911" and "Rain on Me," the latter with Grande as special guest. For good measure, she also won five awards, including Artist of the Year, Song of the Year, Best Cinematography, Best Collaboration for "Rain on Me," and the first-ever Tricon Award, given to artists talented in multiple creative disciplines.

"Rain on Me" also won a Best Pop Duo/Group Performance Grammy—the first time, incredibly enough, a duet with two women won this category—and became yet another global blockbuster chart success, hitting No. 1 in the US and countless other places.

With her proposed Chromatica Ball tour postponed due to the pandemic, Gaga turned to philanthropy, curating the 2020 benefit concert One World: Together at Home, which earned an amazing $127 million for COVID-19 relief efforts. Gaga worked on the fundraiser with multiple people, including her boyfriend, a Harvard graduate and tech entrepreneur named Michael Polansky. The cute couple first went public in early February 2020 via an adorable Instagram photo featuring Gaga curled up in Polansky's lap as he looks at her with an adoring gaze.

During one of the most fraught times in modern history, the optimistic outlook of *Chromatica* ended up inspiring not just Gaga, but the world. "On my new album, I want everyone to know that even if life is painful sometimes, you can still dance through it," she told *Vogue*. "You can dance through it because you're being brave by fighting the pain and living life. This is something that should be celebrated. This is a reason to dance."

CHAPTER TWELVE

RE-BORN
THIS WAY

Although Gaga was off the road in 2020 and into 2021, she was never far from the spotlight. Multiple songs on *Chromatica* were released as remixes, while she became the face of the new Valentino perfume Voce Viva in fall 2020. Gaga and her mom, Cynthia, also co-wrote a book, *Channel Kindness: Stories of Kindness and Community*, that featured more than fifty inspiring stories from young people and spawned a website that gives people a chance to share more moments of kindness.

In early 2021, Gaga also had the honor of singing the National Anthem at the inauguration of the forty-sixth president of the United States, Joe Biden. The day before, she posted a photo of herself in Washington, D.C., wearing a sleek Givenchy white cape dress, alongside a heartfelt wish for tranquility. "I pray tomorrow will be a day of peace for all Americans," she wrote. "A day for love, not hatred. A day for acceptance not fear. A day for dreaming of our future joy as a country. A dream that is non-violent, a dream that provides safety for our souls."

On the actual Inauguration Day, she performed while wearing a subtly patriotic custom outfit designed by Daniel Roseberry: a form-fitting navy cashmere jacket with a gigantic dove brooch and a flowing red silk faille skirt. Her operatic performance was bold and proud, and certainly wowed people who still thought she was "only" a pop star.

Gaga returned to the spotlight in a big way several months later, when West Hollywood, California, christened May 23 as Born This Way Day, with a giant road mural that spelled out the phrase using the rainbow-hued designs of various pride flags. Gaga was on hand

to celebrate in person, sporting a poofy updo, fishnets with giant holes, and bright pink platform boots to accept a key to the city from Mayor Lindsey P. Horvath. "I'm sure this will sound cheesy to some people, not to me, but you've been the motherfucking key to my heart for a long time," Gaga said. "I'll honor this, I'll cherish this, and I promise that I'll always be here for this day."

Her reverence and emotion were genuine. On Instagram, a clearly touched Gaga made sure to bring up the activist Carl Bean, who had inspired "Born This Way," writing in a post, "Thank you for decades of relentless love, bravery, and a reason to sing. So we can all feel joy, because we deserve joy. Because we deserve the right to inspire tolerance, acceptance, and freedom for all."

This celebration was a much-needed bright spot, as in June, Gaga also postponed her Chromatica Ball dates *again*, to summer 2022, due to safety concerns around the ongoing COVID-19 pandemic. As per usual, however, Gaga had things up her sleeve to assuage fan disappointment. She popped up during the much-anticipated reunion special for the nineties sitcom *Friends* and sang a duet with actress Lisa Kudrow. Sporting a nineties-esque, oversized magenta-

ABOVE Arriving to sing the US National Anthem at the inauguration of Joe Biden, 2021.

THE ESSENTIAL... LADY GAGA

and-yellow sweater and a hairdo with tiny braids, she strummed a red acoustic guitar and belted out the show's outsider-folk classic "Smelly Cat" with aplomb. In June, she also had a conversation with Dr. Bernice King, the CEO of The Martin Luther King Jr. Center for Nonviolent Social Change, about the "power of unlearning" and ways to dismantle white supremacy.

A few weeks later, a momentous date in the Gaga-verse arrived: the tenth anniversary of *Born This Way*. Fans and critics alike feted the album as culturally significant. *Buzzfeed* ran a piece, "Here's How Lady Gaga's *Born This Way* Album Has Saved Lives For The Past Decade," rounding up rather moving remembrances from fans about the record's impact, such as, "It captured the essence of the queer experience for me," and, "'The Edge of Glory' really helped me through the death of my grandpa, and it taught me to celebrate life."

Gaga herself celebrated the milestone release of *Born This Way* with a pride-geared Versace capsule collection and a deluxe album reissue featuring a bonus covers EP, *Born This Way Reimagined: The Tenth Anniversary*. In a nod to the record's stature within the LGBTQIA+ community, she chose artists and allies for remakes, including New Orleans bounce legend Big Freedia, pop superstar Kylie Minogue, nu-country star Orville Peck, Broadway star Ben Platt, and Americana superstars The Highwomen.

It was clear this EP was as much a gift to Gaga as it was to fans. "Thank you to each of the incredible artists who reimagined #BornThisWay songs!" she tweeted in celebration. "And thank you, Little Monsters, for building our community of love, acceptance, and kindness for the last 10 years. I'm so grateful for each of you. Rejoice and love yourself today 'cause baby, you were Born This Way."

That wasn't the only positive news: Despite the up-and-down nature of the pandemic, she and Polansky weathered these tough

> "Whenever someone told me I wasn't good enough, I never let it break me. I promised myself that every time I heard 'no,' it would motivate me to work harder."

times. "Michael is her North Star," a source told *Entertainment Tonight*, adding, "He is such a grounding and guiding presence for her." Perhaps even more important, the source noted, "He loves Lady Gaga, but he's in love with Stefani." As of spring 2024, the couple was still going strong.

Her postponed Chromatica Ball tour launched in July 2022. It was worth the wait: Grossing $112.4 million from more than 800,000 tickets sold, it also spawned a 2024 HBO Original concert special, *Gaga Chromatica Ball*.

Furthermore, Gaga co-wrote the song "Hold My Hand" for the 2022 film *Top Gun: Maverick*—the tune earned an Oscar nod for Best Original Song—and collaborated on the score with composition icons Hans Zimmer and Harold Faltermeyer. And in 2023, President Joe Biden appointed Gaga as co-chair of the President's Committee on the Arts and Humanities. Later in the year, she collaborated with rockers The Rolling Stones on their barn-burning new song, "Sweet Sounds of Heaven." For good measure, Gaga also landed a co-starring role with Joaquin Phoenix in the high-profile 2024 movie *Joker: Folie à Deux*.

Gaga makes balancing movie and music careers look easy; in hindsight, it's easy to see how she could've pursued acting instead. However, we're lucky she chose songwriting and performing, as the modern pop world would be completely different had Gaga not become a success. She not only brought weirdness back into the mainstream—and taught multiple generations of fans and artists to embrace their oddball quirks—she also built bridges between scenes and genres: New York downtown punk, sophisticated club

THE ESSENTIAL... LADY GAGA

THE ESSENTIAL... LADY GAGA

culture, ecstatic dancefloor electro, grimy dive-bar rock, arena-epic classic rock.

Gaga herself has grown and evolved during her time in the spotlight. The scrappy resilience she displayed early on in her career has blossomed into something more enduring—a steely resolve of personal strength and emotional generosity. "Whenever someone told me I wasn't good enough throughout my career and life, I never let it break me," she told *Vogue* in October 2020. "I promised myself that every time I heard 'no,' it would motivate me to work harder."

Where she goes next will be anyone's guess, although what's a little easier to pin down is her legacy. She's set the musical bar high for her pop peers (including Katy Perry, Miley Cyrus, Demi Lovato, and Ellie Goulding) and has been a role model for a new generation of trendsetters: pop wizard Charli XCX, dancefloor queens Slayyyter and Dua Lipa, and the genre-blending Olivia Rodrigo and Chappell Roan. Lady Gaga's longevity is a testament not only to her talent, but also her open-hearted nature and brilliant foresight.

The Fame (2008)

Track List (US standard edition):

1. Just Dance (*featuring Colby O'Donis*)
2. LoveGame
3. Paparazzi
4. Poker Face
5. Eh, Eh (Nothing Else I Can Say)
6. Beautiful, Dirty, Rich
7. The Fame
8. Money Honey
9. Starstruck (*featuring Space Cowboy and Flo Rida*)
10. Boys Boys Boys
11. Paper Gangsta
12. Brown Eyes
13. I Like It Rough
14. Summerboy

Recorded

150 (Parsippany-Troy Hills, NJ); 333 (New York City, NY); Chalice (Los Angeles, CA); Cherrytree (Santa Monica, CA); Dojo (New York City, NY); Poe Boy (Miami, FL); Record Plant (Los Angeles, CA)

Released

October 28, 2008 (US), January 12, 2009 (UK)

Label

Streamline/KonLive/Cherrytree/Interscope

Notes

The Fame had different release dates in various territories throughout 2008 and 2009. Many of these versions also had different bonus tracks, depending on the country of release. For example, the Japanese editions had the disco-rock anthem "Retro Dance Freak," while "Disco Heaven" was a bonus track on the UK standard version. Rapper Flo Rida also appears on "Starstruck."

The Fame Monster (2009)

Track List
1. Bad Romance
2. Alejandro
3. Monster
4. Speechless
5. Dance In The Dark
6. Telephone
7. So Happy I Could Die
8. Teeth

Recorded
Darkchild Studios (Los Angeles, CA); FC Walvisch (Amsterdam, Netherlands); Metropolis Studios (London, UK); Record Plant (Los Angeles, CA); Studio Groove (Osaka, Japan)

Released
November 23, 2009 (US & UK)

Label
Streamline/KonLive/Cherrytree/Interscope

Notes
The Fame Monster was issued as an EP appended to *The Fame* but was also released in multiple different versions around the world in 2009 and 2010, including as a stand-alone release. For example, a super deluxe version included some hair from an actual Gaga wig, while a USB edition featured re-dos and remixes, such as "LoveGame (Robots To Mars Remix)."

In 2010 Gaga released a remix album combining songs from *The Fame* and *The Fame Monster,* titled *The Remix*. Issued on May 4 in the UK and August 3 in the US, the full-length featured a Passion Pit remix of "Telephone" and a Stuart Price re-do of "Paparazzi."

OPPOSITE
Supporting the Pussycat Dolls on their world tour, 2009.

Born This Way (2011)

Track List
1. Marry The Night
2. Born This Way
3. Government Hooker
4. Judas
5. Americano
6. Hair
7. Scheiße
8. Bloody Mary
9. Bad Kids
10. Highway Unicorn (Road To Love)
11. Heavy Metal Lover
12. Electric Chapel
13. Yoü And I
14. The Edge Of Glory

Recorded
Abbey Road Studios (London, UK); Allertown Hill (London, UK); Gang Studios (Paris, France); Germano Studios (New York City, NY); Officine Mechaniche Studios (Milano, Italy); Paradise Studios (Hollywood, CA); Studios 301 (Sydney, Australia); Studio at the Palms (Las Vegas, NV); Studio Bus (mobile tour bus recording studio); The Living Room Studios (Oslo, Norway); The Mix Room (Burbank, CA); Warehouse Productions (Omaha, NE)

Released
May 23, 2011

Label
Streamline/KonLive/Interscope Records

Notes
The album sold an incredible 1.1 million copies in its first week on sale in the US. Globally, there were also different versions of *Born This Way* released, including one featuring the bonus track "Black Jesus + Amen Fashion." On November 21, 2011, Gaga released her second remix album, *Born This Way: The Remix*, in the US and UK. The full-length featured remixes of songs by Goldfrapp, The Weeknd, Zedd, and Twin Shadow, among others.

OPPOSITE
At the 2011 Grammy Awards.

ARTPOP (2013)

Track List

1. Aura
2. Venus
3. G.U.Y.
4. Sexxx Dreams
5. Jewels N' Drugs
   (*featuring T.I., Too $hort and Twista*)
6. MANiCURE
7. Do What U Want
   (*featuring R. Kelly*)
8. Artpop
9. Swine
10. Donatella
11. Fashion!
12. Mary Jane Holland
13. Dope
14. Gypsy
15. Applause

Recorded

80 Hertz Studios (Manchester, UK); CRC Studios (Chicago, IL); Patchwerk Studios (Atlanta, GA); Piano Music Studios (Amsterdam, NL); Platinum Sound Recording Studios (New York City, NY); Record Plant (Los Angeles, CA); Shangri-La Studios (Malibu, CA)

Released

November 11, 2013

Label

Streamline/Interscope

Notes

Rappers T.I., Twista, Too $hort, and R. Kelly appear, as does Rick Rubin. One-time Whitesnake and Dio guitarist Doug Aldrich plays on "MANiCURE," while guitarist Tim Stewart, who has played with Infectious Grooves, also contributes to several songs.

Cheek to Cheek
(with Tony Bennett) (2014)

Track List
1. Anything Goes
2. Cheek To Cheek
3. Nature Boy
4. I Can't Give You Anything But Love
5. I Won't Dance
6. Firefly
7. Lush Life
8. Sophisticated Lady
9. Let's Face The Music And Dance
10. But Beautiful
11. It Don't Mean A Thing (If It Ain't Got That Swing)

Recorded
Avatar Studio C (New York City, NY); Kaufman Astoria Studios (Astoria, New York City, NY); Manhattan Center Studios (New York City, NY)

Released
September 22, 2014 (UK); September 23, 2014 (US)

Label
Columbia/Streamline/Interscope

Notes
The album is a collaboration with the legendary crooner Tony Bennett. Bennett and Gaga used a variety of session jazz musicians, including members of Bennett's band, for the recording. With this album, Lady Gaga became the first female solo artist to have three No. 1 US albums in the 2010s. Tony Bennett also extended his record as the oldest artist to have a No. 1 album.

OPPOSITE
Lady Gaga and Tony Bennett, 2015.

Joanne (2016)

Track List

1. Diamond Heart
2. A-YO
3. Joanne
4. John Wayne
5. Dancin' In Circles
6. Perfect Illusion
7. Million Reasons
8. Sinner's Prayer
9. Come To Mama
10. Hey Girl (*featuring Florence Welch*)
11. Angel Down

Recorded

123 Studios (London, UK); Diamond Mine Recording Co. (New York City, NY); Dragonfly Recording Studios (Malibu, CA); Electric Lady Studios (New York City, NY); The Farm (London, UK); GenPop Laboratory (Los Angeles, CA); Green Oak Studios (Los Angeles, CA); Gypsy Palace (Malibu, CA); Pink Duck Studios (Burbank, CA); Shangri-La Studios (Malibu, CA); Vox Recording Studios (Los Angeles, CA); Zelig (London, UK)

Released

October 21, 2016

Label

Streamline/Interscope

Notes

Joanne was a departure for Gaga, as the album toned down the dance-oriented electronic flourishes in favor of more personal, introspective songwriting. The death of Gaga's aunt Joanne Stefani Germanotta deeply influenced the album. Florence Welch sings on and co-wrote "Hey Girl," while the album also features contributions from Josh Homme, Beck Hansen, and Tame Impala's Kevin Parker.

A Star is Born Soundtrack (2018)

Track List
1. Black Eyes
2. La Vie En Rose
3. Maybe It's Time
4. Out Of Time
5. Alibi
6. Shallow
7. Music To My Eyes
8. Diggin' My Grave
9. Always Remember Us This Way
10. Look What I Found
11. Heal Me
12. I Don't Know What Love Is
13. Is That Alright?
14. Why Did You Do That?
15. Hair Body Face
16. Before I Cry
17. Too Far Gone
18. I'll Never Love Again *(Film Version)*
19. I'll Never Love Again *(Extended Version)*

Recorded
EastWest Studios (Los Angeles, CA); Electric Lady Studios (New York City, NY); Shangri-La Studios (Malibu, CA); The Village West (Los Angeles, CA); Woodrow Wilson Studios (Hollywood, CA)

Released
October 5, 2018

Label
Interscope

Notes
Actor Bradley Cooper contributed songwriting, production, and vocals, while Willie Nelson's son, Lukas Nelson, and Nashville producer Dave Cobb also contributed. The soundtrack became Gaga's longest-running No. 1 album in the US, as the LP debuted at the top of the chart and spent three consecutive weeks at the peak, and later returned to the top spot for a fourth week. The *A Star Is Born* soundtrack also spent ten weeks atop the Australian album charts.

OPPOSITE
Singing with Bradley Cooper in *A Star Is Born*, 2018.

Chromatica (2020)

Track List
1. Chromatica I
2. Alice
3. Stupid Love
4. Rain On Me (*featuring Ariana Grande*)
5. Free Woman
6. Fun Tonight
7. Chromatica II
8. 911
9. Plastic Doll
10. Sour Candy (*featuring Blackpink*)
11. Enigma
12. Replay
13. Chromatica III
14. Sine From Above (*featuring Elton John*)
15. 1000 Doves
16. Babylon

Recorded
Conway Recording (Hollywood, CA); EastWest (Hollywood, CA); Electric Lady (New York City, NY); Sterling Sound (New York City, NY); Good Father (Los Angeles, CA); Henson Recording (Los Angeles, CA); MXM Studios (Los Angeles, CA); Utility Muffin Research Kitchen (Hollywood Hills, CA)

Released
May 29, 2020

Label
Streamline/Interscope

Notes
Elton John sings on and co-wrote "Sine From Above"; Ariana Grande sings on and co-wrote "Rain On Me"; Blackpink appears on "Sour Candy." *Chromatica* has additional bonus tracks for other territories, including alternate versions of "Stupid Love" and "1000 Doves." On September 3, 2021, Gaga released her third remix album, *Dawn of Chromatica*. The effort featured re-dos of *Chromatica* tunes by Charli XCX, Rina Sawayama, Planningtorock, and Shygirl and Mura Masa.

Love For Sale
(with Tony Bennett) (2021)

Track List

1. It's De-Lovely
2. Night And Day
3. Love For Sale
4. Do I Love You
5. I Concentrate On You
6. I Get A Kick Out Of You
7. So In Love
8. Let's Do It (Let's Fall In Love)
9. Just One Of Those Things
10. Dream Dancing

Recorded
Electric Lady Studios (New York City, NY)

Released
October 1, 2021 (worldwide)

Label
Streamline/Columbia/Interscope

Notes
Bennett's final album. He sings two solo songs, "So In Love" and "Just One Of Those Things," while Gaga solos on "Do I Love You" and "Let's Do It (Let's Fall In Love)." Grammy Award-winning composer Jorge Calandrelli arranged and conducted the orchestra. The release of *Love For Sale* saw Bennett break the Guinness World Record for the oldest person to release an album of new material, at the age of ninety-five years and sixty days. *Love For Sale* was a family affair: Dae Bennett, who produced the album, is Tony Bennett's son. Danny Bennett, Tony's oldest son and long-time manager, also contributed, as did Danny's daughter and Tony's granddaughter, Kelsey Bennett, who oversaw photography.

OPPOSITE
Lady Gaga, 2021.

SOURCES

www.aarp.org; www.abcnews.go.com; www.apnews.com; www.bbc.com; www.billboard.com; www.bornthisway. foundation; www.buzzfeed.com; www.capradio.org; www.cbsnews.com; www.completemusicupdate.com; www. dailymail.co.uk; www.dailystar.co.uk; www.eonline.com; www.elle.com; www.ew.com; www.factmag.com; www. findagrave.com; www.forbes.com; www.harpersbazaar.com; www.herworld.com; www.hollywoodreporter.com; www.huffpost.com; www.ibtimes.com; www.independent.co.uk; www.independent.ie; www.insider.com; www.instyle. com; www.ladygaga.fandom.com; www.lamaisongaga.com; www.metacritic.com; www.mtv.com; www.music-news. com; www.nbcbayarea.com; www.newspapers.com; www.newsweek.com;www.nme.com; www.nycago.org; www.nydailynews.com; www.nymag.com; www.nypost.com; www.nytimes.com; www.nyuirhc.org; www.observer. com; www.out.com; www.papermag.com; www.people.com; www.popcrush.com; www.pri.org; www.racked.com; www.rollingstone.com; www.scifivision.com; www.today.com; www.thedailybeast.com; www.thefader.com; www. theguardian.com; www.time.com; www.twitter.com; www.undergroundfairy.blogspot.com; www.usmagazine.com; www.usatoday.com; www.variety.com; www.versace.com; www.vice.com; www.vogue.com; www.web.archive.org; www.en.wikipedia.org; www.wkyc.com; www.wwd.com; www.youtube.com; www.yahoo.com

PICTURE CREDITS

T: Top; B: Bottom; L: Left; R: Right

ALAMY: COVER: PictureLux /The Hollywood Archive **P6** Doug Peters **P11, P125** LANDMARK MEDIA **P24** AP Photo/Peter Kramer **P28B** Wendy Connett **P32-33** Chaz Niell/Southcreek EMI/ZUMA Press **P40** Pictorial Press Ltd **P51T, P60, P66B, P88T, P95** WENN Rights Ltd **P56** NBC-TV/Album **P58** The Photo Access **P66T** Album/Alamy Stock Photo **P72** Abaca Press/Alamy Stock Photo **P74** Olivier Douliery/ABACAPRESS.COM **P76, P80T** Imaginechina Limited/Alamy Stock Photo **P84** REUTERS/Lucas Jackson **P86** REUTERS/Toru Hana **P100-101** BBC/Album **P104** Derek Storm/Everett Collection/ Alamy Live New **P124TL** Photo 12/Alamy Stock Photo **P124TR** Collection Christophel/Alamy Stock Photo **P129** Metro-Goldwyn-Mayer (MGM)/Album/Alamy Stock Photo **P136** REUTERS/Marco Bello **P142** Luke Durda/Alamy Stock Photo **P148** dpa picture alliance/Alamy Live News **P166** Marco Piraccini/Mondadori Portfolio/Sipa USA **P170** APL Archive/Alamy Stock Photo **GETTY 8T** Gareth Cattermole **P8BL, P88B, P102, P116** Kevin Mazur **P8BR** Theo Wargo **P9, P68, P69, P103, P106-107, P127B** Kevin Winter **P12** Chelsea Lauren/WireImage **P14** Larry Busacca/ Getty Images for Giorgio Armani **P17T, P36** Jason Squires/WireImage **P17B, P51B, P57** Kevin Mazur/WireImage **P18L** Chris Gabrin/Redferns **P18R** Paul Bergen/Redferns **P20-21** ANDREAS BRANCH/Patrick McMullan via Getty Images **P26, P34-35** Theo Wargo/WireImage **P29** Eric CATARINA/Gamma-Rapho via Getty Images **P30L** Monica Schipper **P30R** L. Busacca/WireImage for Songwriter's Hall of Fame **P38, P44-45** Roger Kisby **P41** D. Kambouris / WireImage **P42** Eugene Gologursky/WireImage **P43** John Medina/WireImage **P46** Jeff Fusco **P50** Weegee(Arthur Fellig)/International Center of Photography **P52** Christopher Polk **P53** Dave M. Benett **P62** Jason Merritt **P63T** Ollie Millington/Redferns **P63B** Michael Caulfield/WireImage **P70** Visual China Group via Getty Images **P75** Gie Knaeps **P77T** ALBERTO PIZZOLI/ AFP via Getty Images **P77B** Hamid Mousa-Cool Kids Club **P78** Christopher Polk/Getty Images for Children's Mending Hearts **P79** Tim Greenway/Portland Press Herald via Getty Images **P80B** Anthony Harvey **P82** Chelsea Lauren **P87, P165** Kevin Mazur/WireImage **P89** Dimitrios Kambouris **P90** Kevin Mazur/AMA2013/WireImage **P91, P92-93** Christopher Polk/WireImage **P96** Jeff Kravitz/WireImage **P98** Kevin Mazur/Getty Images for Citi **P105** Kevin Mazur/ Getty Images for RPM **P108, P118-119** Patrick Smith **P110, P117, P150-151, P154** Kevin Mazur/Getty Images for Live Nation **P112** Francis Specker/CBS via Getty Images **P113TL** James Devaney/WireImage **P113TR** Jun Sato/WireImage **P113B** James Keivom/New York Daily News **P114T** MARK RALSTON/AFP via Getty Images **P114B** Scott Legato/Getty Images for Live Nation **P122** FILIPPO MONTEFORTE/AFP via Getty Images **P130-131** Matt Petit-Handout/A.M.P.A.S. via Getty Images **P132** Theo Wargo/Getty Images for AT&T **P134** Kevin Mazur/Getty Images for Park MGM Las Vegas **P137, P139, P140-141, P143T&B, P173** Kevin Winter/MTV VMAs 2020/Getty Images for MTV **P138** Jason Koerner/Getty Images for Oprah **P144** Samir Hussein **P146** Jeff Kravitz/Getty Images for Live Nation **P149** Dimitrios Kambouris/Getty Images for National Board of Review **P152-153** Kevin Mazur/Getty Images for RS **P155** Raymond Hall/GC Images **P156-157** Rodin Eckenroth **P158** Kevin Mazur/WireImage for Clear Channel **P161** Jakubaszek **P169** James Devaney/ GC Images **SHUTTERSTOCK P4** Paul Grover **P10** Invision/AP **P22-23** Ronald Wittek/EPA **P48** Erik Pendzich **P54** Brendan Beirne **P64-65** Nam Y Huh/AP **P115** Buzz Foto **P120** David Fisher **P127T** Prashant Gupta/Fx/Kobal **P162** Matt Sayles/AP **P174** Christopher Polk

THE ESSENTIAL... LADY GAGA